THE CITIES OF THE FUTURE

DIDIER CORNILLE

Translated by Charis Ainslie

post wave

Join   Didier Cornille   on a tour of the

world's greatest   cities!

Cities Are Amazing!

They are full of bright lights, incredible sights and thousands of people adding to the hustle and bustle. But cities can also feel chaotic, with too many people searching for space to share, too much traffic and pollution and not enough green spaces for city dwellers to enjoy and connect with nature.

Today, half of the world's population lives in cities — and by 2050 this will rise to four in every five people. We need to think about how we can solve the problems that make life in cities difficult, and how we can create a culture that means city living is not only possible and sustainable, but also enjoyable.

Many cities around the world are dreaming up new ways of living, and some of them have had surprisingly good results. So, why not take inspiration from them to help design the Cities of the Future?

With this book in your hands, you can dream about the kind of city you'd like to live in. And maybe, one day, you'll help build it!

In the 1970s, as the world's population grew, large numbers of people flocked to cities to find jobs.

Cities became vast and sprawling, fed by busy roads carrying chaotic traffic and criss-crossed by cyclists and pedestrians.

Slowly, they spread further and further, eating into the countryside, threatening nature and pumping out pollution.

If you can't build outwards, build upwards! To create homes and workplaces for everyone, skyscrapers that reached dizzying heights were built.

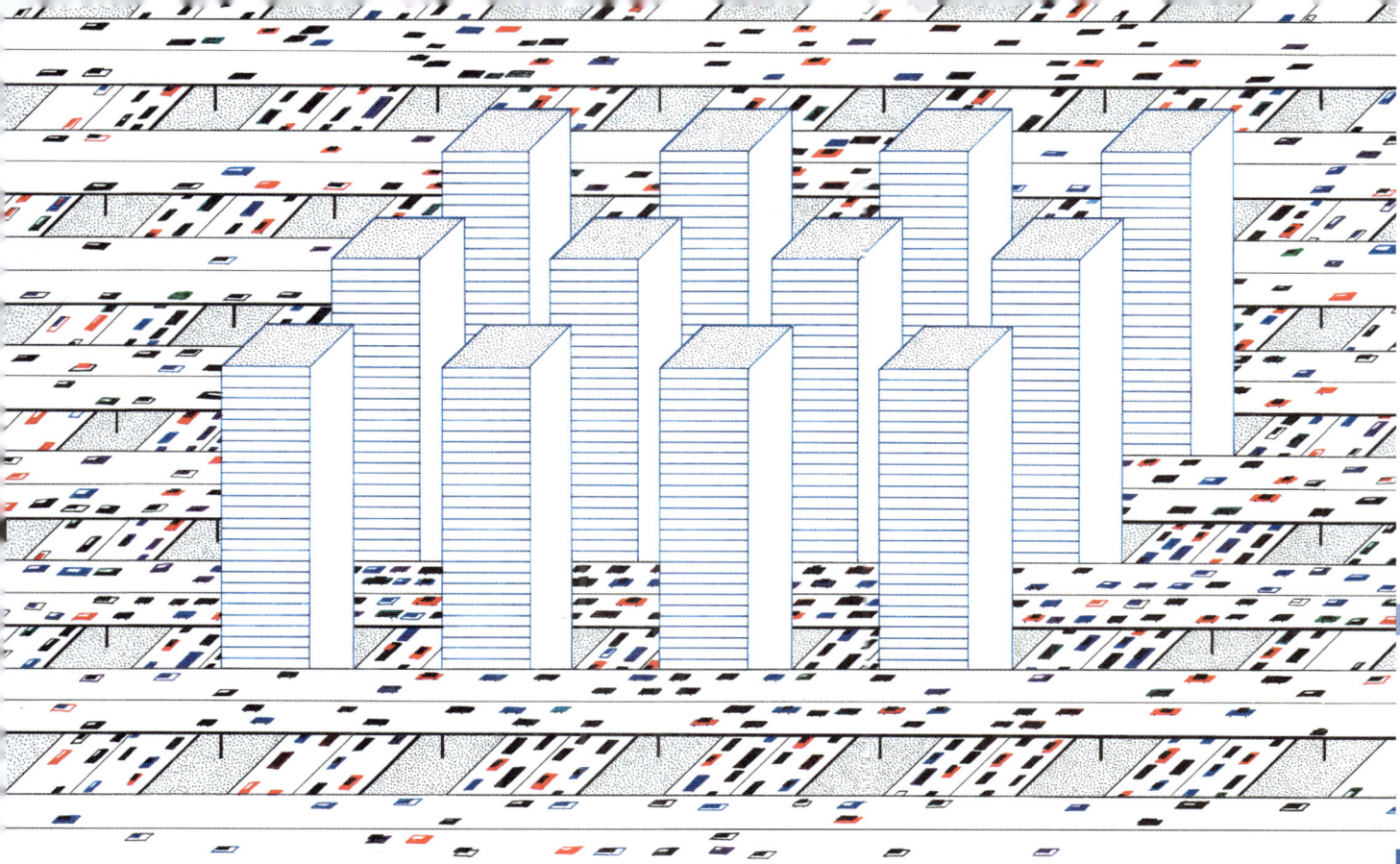

In other areas, makeshift communities sprang up. The people who lived there were very poor and built houses out of whatever they could find. Life in these areas could be difficult, but neighbours often supported each other.

It raised the question: how can we tackle poverty in cities?

Suburbs grew around the cities – often in the shape of large housing estates. Although cheap to build, these homes were often a long way from the city centres where people worked and lived.

People living in the suburbs need homes, as well as schools, medical facilities and a good transport network, along with places to relax, exercise and have fun.

In other areas of the suburbs, there are rows and rows of houses that all look the same, each with a tiny garden.

To get from one suburb to another, or to reach the centre of town, people must drive or catch a bus.

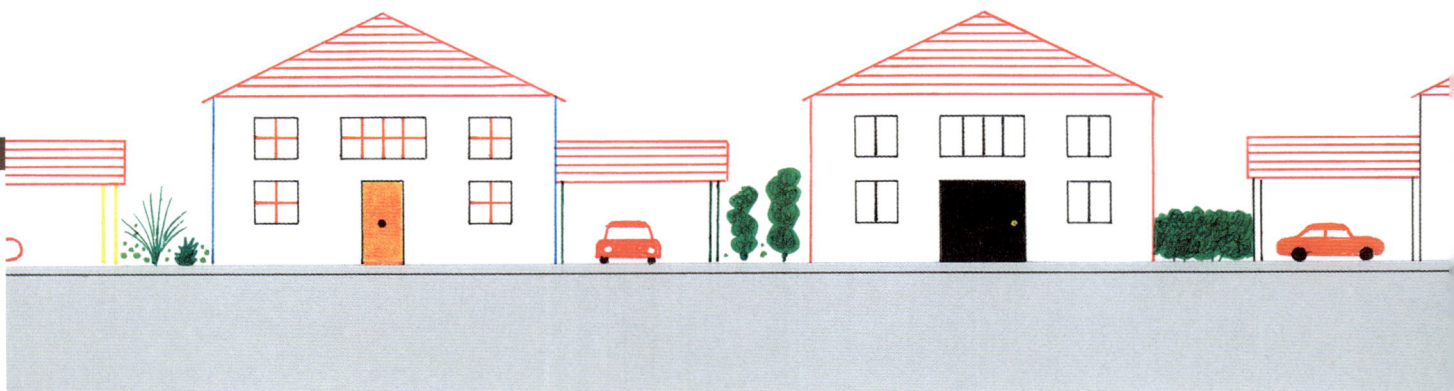

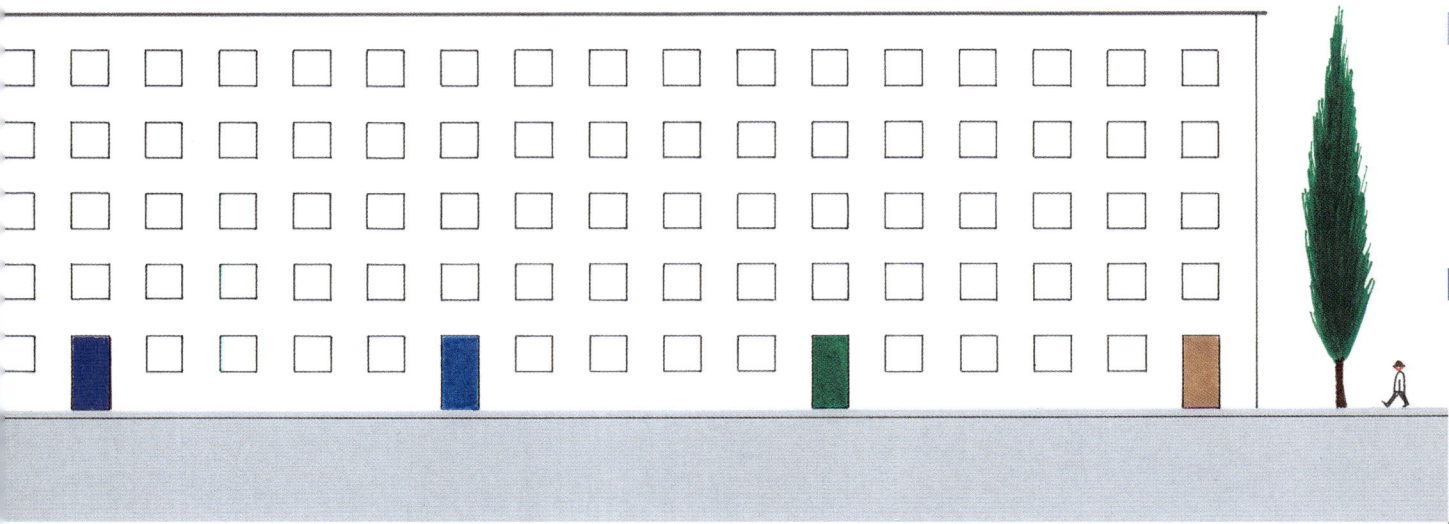

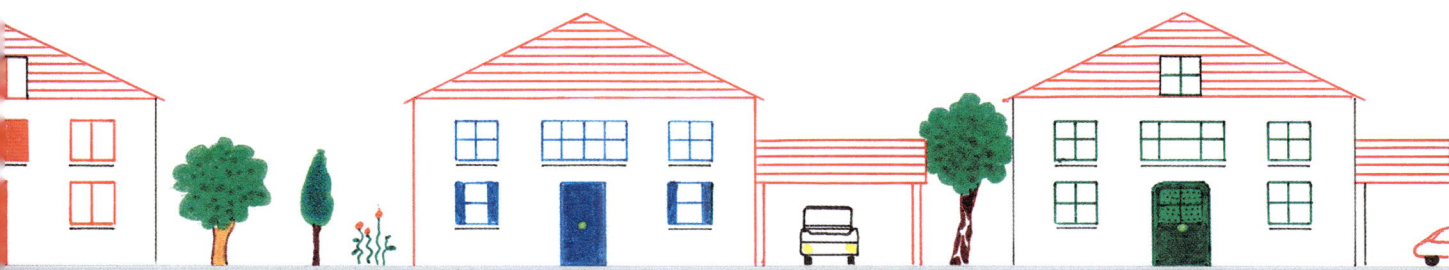

Could Our Cities Be Greener?

Heavy traffic, central heating, air conditioning and smoke from factories causes pollution in our cities. This has contributed to rising temperatures across the planet.

How can we provide clean air for the people who live in cities and are faced with this pollution every day? The answer is clear – we need to bring nature into our cities!

MARSEILLE: A VERTICAL CITY

Cross section of The Housing Unit, Marseille, France

Architect: Le Corbusier (1952)

In the 1930s, the architect Charles-Édouard Jeanneret, known as Le Corbusier, came up with a design for an ingenious modern town that could be built anywhere in the world. His idea was to group homes together in housing estates, keeping cars and pedestrians separate and protecting green spaces.

The Radiant City was built in Marseille, France, in 1952 and was part of the reconstruction that took place after the Second World War. It is a tall concrete building stood on stilts. Outside, it is surrounded by a park; inside, there are 360 apartments, most of which have two floors. They fit together on 'streets' inside the building.

On top of the building is a roof terrace with a sunroom and a running track around the edge. Halfway up the building, there's a shopping centre with a bakery, shops and even a hotel. A school, a gym, a stage, a paddling pool and several children's play areas complete the design – not forgetting the incredible views from the top of this vertical city!

Le Corbusier designed similar projects in other towns in France and elsewhere in Europe, as well as in India.

CHANDIGARH: A MODERN TOWN FOR OUTDOOR LIVING

Relaxing in Sector 23, Chandigarh, India
Architect: Pierre Jeanneret (1958)

In 1947, India gained its independence. Le Corbusier and his cousin, Pierre Jeanneret, were invited to build a new capital in the Indian state of Punjab.

The cousins observed that people in India lived more outside than in, spending their time on terraces, under colonnades and in gardens. With this in mind, they proposed a new version of the Radiant City, this time with homes arranged in a low, horizontal design.

15

Berlin

16

BERLIN: LEADING THE WAY IN ECOLOGY

Berlin is one of Europe's greenest capitals. Home to millions of people, this huge city in Germany is surrounded by vast forests and criss-crossed by rivers and canals.

Since 1910, Berlin has created lots of green spaces within the city, along with a ring of parks around the outside using a method called 'urban planning'.

Trees were planted along the riverbanks in the 1980s and pleasant pathways were created to link parks together. Not only did this provide a nice environment for the people living there, but it also created a permanent habitat for plants and animals.

Since 2004, the city has been making changes to tackle climate change: new buildings are more spread out, there are more green spaces and air circulation has been improved to keep the city cool.

And that's not all. Residents have been coming up with their own ideas, too. Berliners really care about their city – they've set up communal gardens for everyone to share, worked together to design new green spaces and even created pop-up gardens!

Berlin is a city made by the people, for the people.

THE GLEISDREIECK PARK

This large park was created on the site of a disused railway station not far from the centre of Berlin. The old railway tracks have been replaced with plants and greenery. Local residents have helped to set up outdoor activities that everyone can enjoy.

Park am Gleisdreieck, Berlin, Germany
Landscapers: Atelier LOIDL (2014)

The private gardens that once ran alongside the railway tracks remain the same.

Children play under the railway bridge near the new housing.

The Panke is a little river that runs through Berlin.
Once hidden underground, it has now been uncovered and the
banks have been transformed into a lovely place to walk or rest.

The walls of the apartments nearby are covered in a thick coat of
leaves, keeping the buildings cool in the summer and warm in the
winter. There's even a little farm where children can pet the animals.

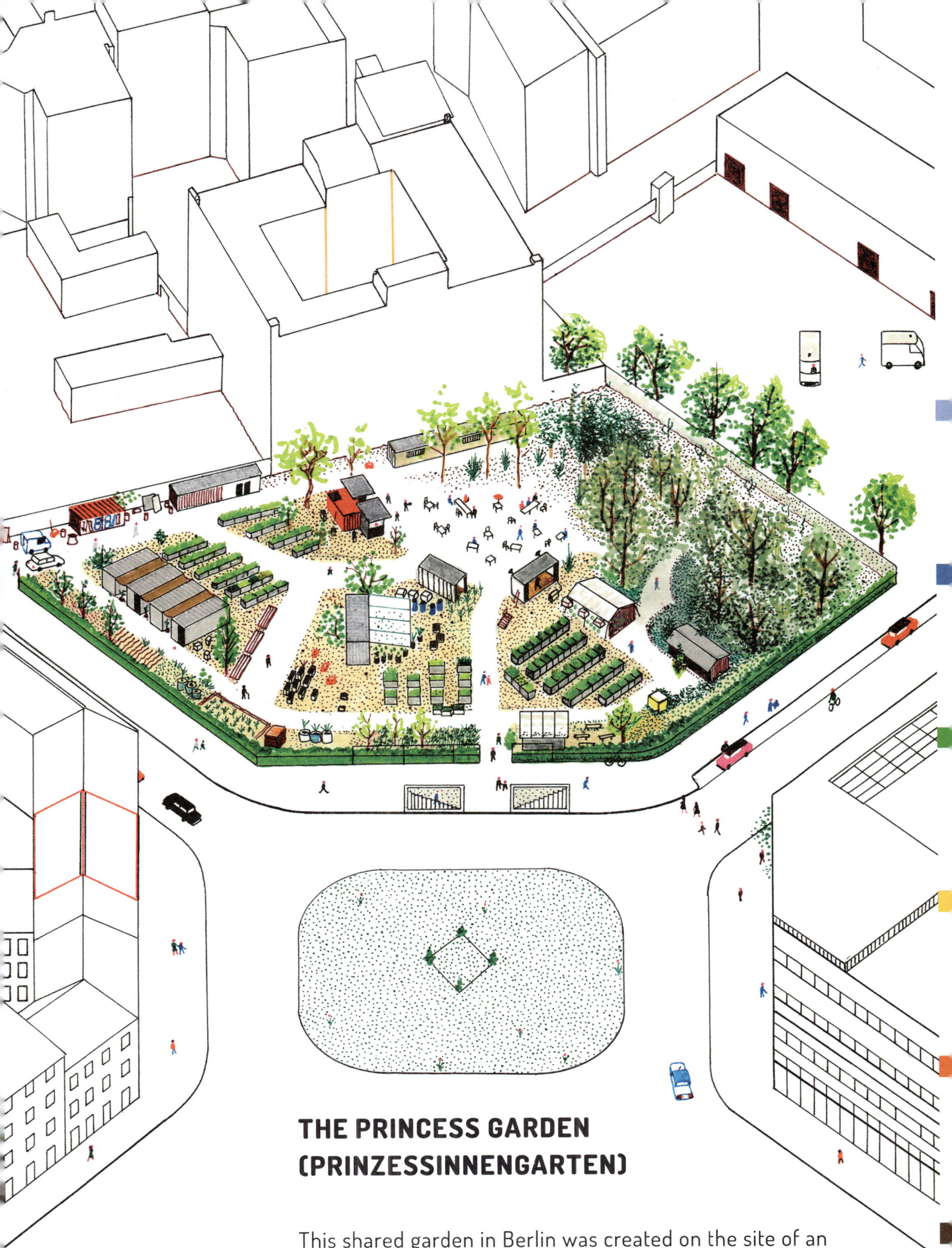

THE PRINCESS GARDEN
(PRINZESSINNENGARTEN)

This shared garden in Berlin was created on the site of an abandoned cemetery in 2009. It has mobile vegetable patches and shows local residents how much fun gardening can be.

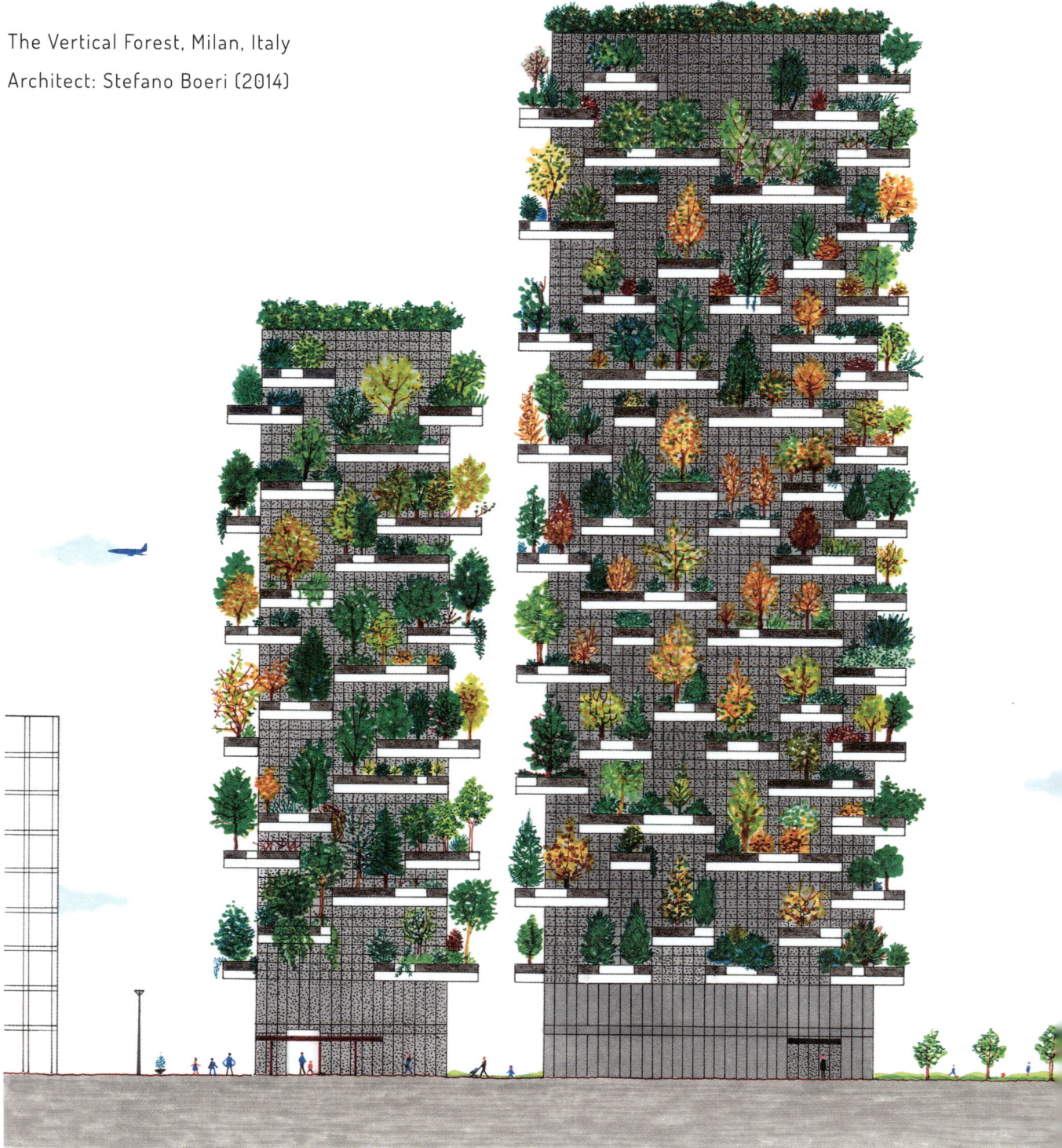

The Vertical Forest, Milan, Italy

Architect: Stefano Boeri (2014)

MILAN: NATURE MAKES A COMEBACK

Italian architect Stefano Boeri believes that a city that keeps growing threatens our planet by destroying natural resources and making life for plants and animals almost impossible. To fix this, he believes we should bring nature back into our cities.

In 2014, two and a half acres of forest were planted on the sides of two high-rise towers, known as the Vertical Forest, in Milan, Italy. Boeri carefully selected the trees and shrubs for the balconies. The Vertical Forest has become a refuge for insects and birds, restoring biodiversity by bringing different types of wildlife back to the city.

The Biomilano
Project
Expo 2015,
Milan, Italy

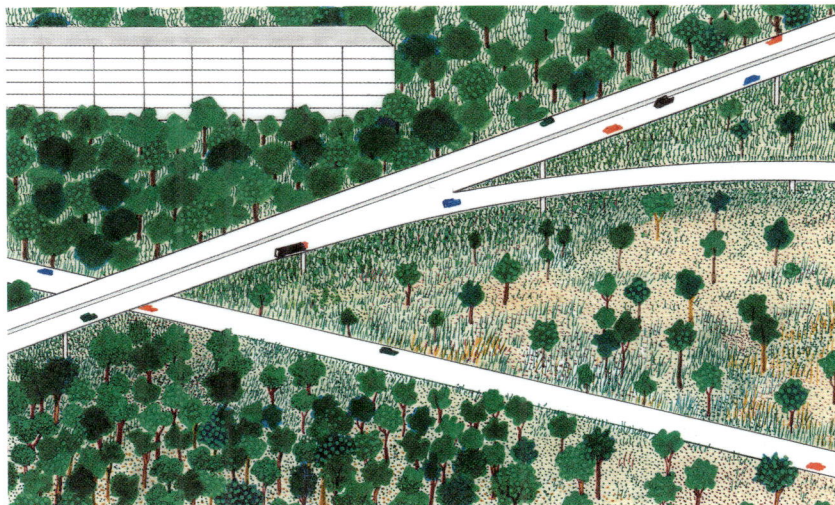

The same architect was behind the Biomilano Project. The aim was to connect Milan's parks and plant greenery around its ring roads – surrounding the city with forest. They hoped this would encourage the animals that had been driven away to return.

Can We Grow Food In Cities?

Why does our food come from so far away when we could raise animals and grow our own food in the city?

THE RAILWAY FARM: HOW TO GROW GREEN

The idea to set up a farm in Paris came from architect Clara Simay. In 2019, the Railway Farm opened on a plot of land in the north-east of the city. The farm experiments with different kinds of urban farming and is open to visitors. It's also a school for gardeners of the future.

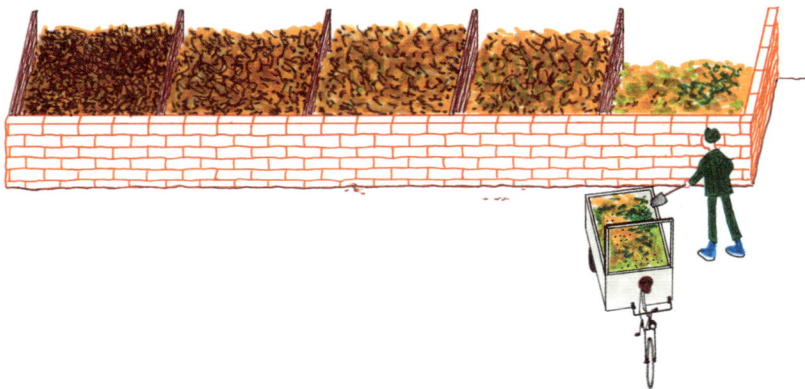

The farm collects leftover food from local restaurants to use as compost. When it's composted, it turns into humus – a dark substance that helps keep the soil healthy.

The Railway Farm site in the north-east of Paris, France

Architect: Clara Simay (2019)

The Railway Farm uses a method of farming called permaculture. This means farmers work with nature by planting crops that help each other grow. Everything is planted in small beds and covered with straw to protect it. The different plants work together to fertilise the soil, prevent pests and retain moisture.

Growing plants in bags means that all types of space can be used – even balconies.

Using a system called aquaponics, the plants are fertilised with waste water from fish farming. The water is rich in carbon dioxide which helps plants grow. It is piped directly from the tanks to the plants. The plants filter it and put oxygen back in, then the water is ready to be used for the fish again.

There are also plans for a greenhouse for exotic fruits and vegetables that need warmer temperatures to grow. This will be attached to a little restaurant serving products grown on the farm.

Last, but not least, there will be a shop where visitors can buy fruit and vegetables to take home.

29

ECOBOXES: POP-UP GARDENS

Farming in towns has led to fascinating inventions that are both practical and clever. ECObox is a system of wooden pallets that can be laid out in spaces that aren't being used – like old car parks or dead-end roads. They transform these spaces into gardens without having to dig up the ground. The result? Pop-up vegetable patches!

The ECObox garden, Paris, France
Architects: AAA (Ateliers d'architecture autogérée) (2005)

DETROIT'S GARDENS: SAVING A STRUGGLING CITY

In the bustling city of Detroit, USA, the car industry was struggling with foreign competition, oil crises and a recession. The factories were forced to close, leaving many people unemployed and large areas deserted.

Some people left in search of better opportunities, but those who remained created community gardens on the industrial wasteland left by the factories. Residents were encouraged to grow their own food which meant that neighbours got to know one another better and all residents got to eat healthy, home-grown food.

An 'agrihood' in the North End neighbourhood of Detroit in the United States (2016)

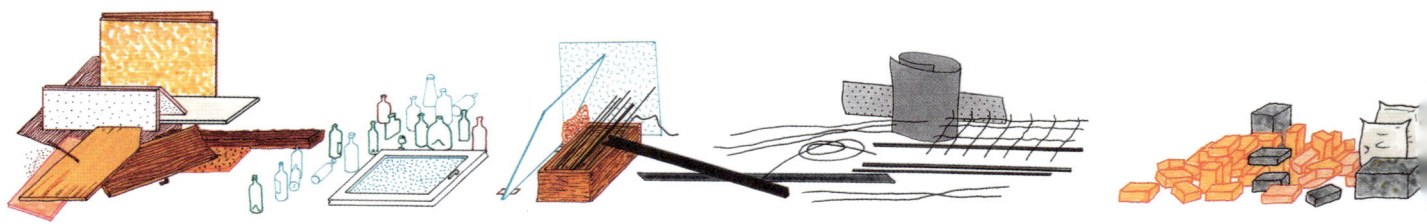

Could We Use Local Materials and Renewable Energy?

An ecodistrict is a town that's built using local materials and powered by renewable energy. The inhabitants adopt a way of living that's better for the planet. Ecodistricts have less of an impact on the environment and allow people to make a difference within their community.

35

BEDZED: KING OF THE ECODISTRICTS

This housing development in south London used exciting new ideas for building homes and revolutionised the way people lived.

BedZED. London, UK (2002)
Architect: Bill Dunster

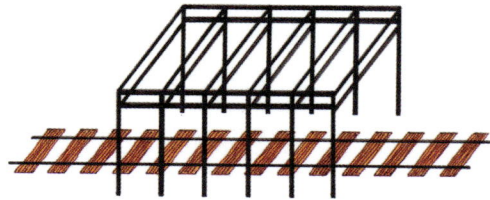

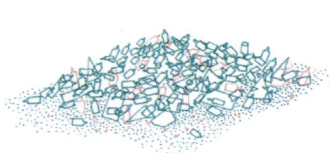

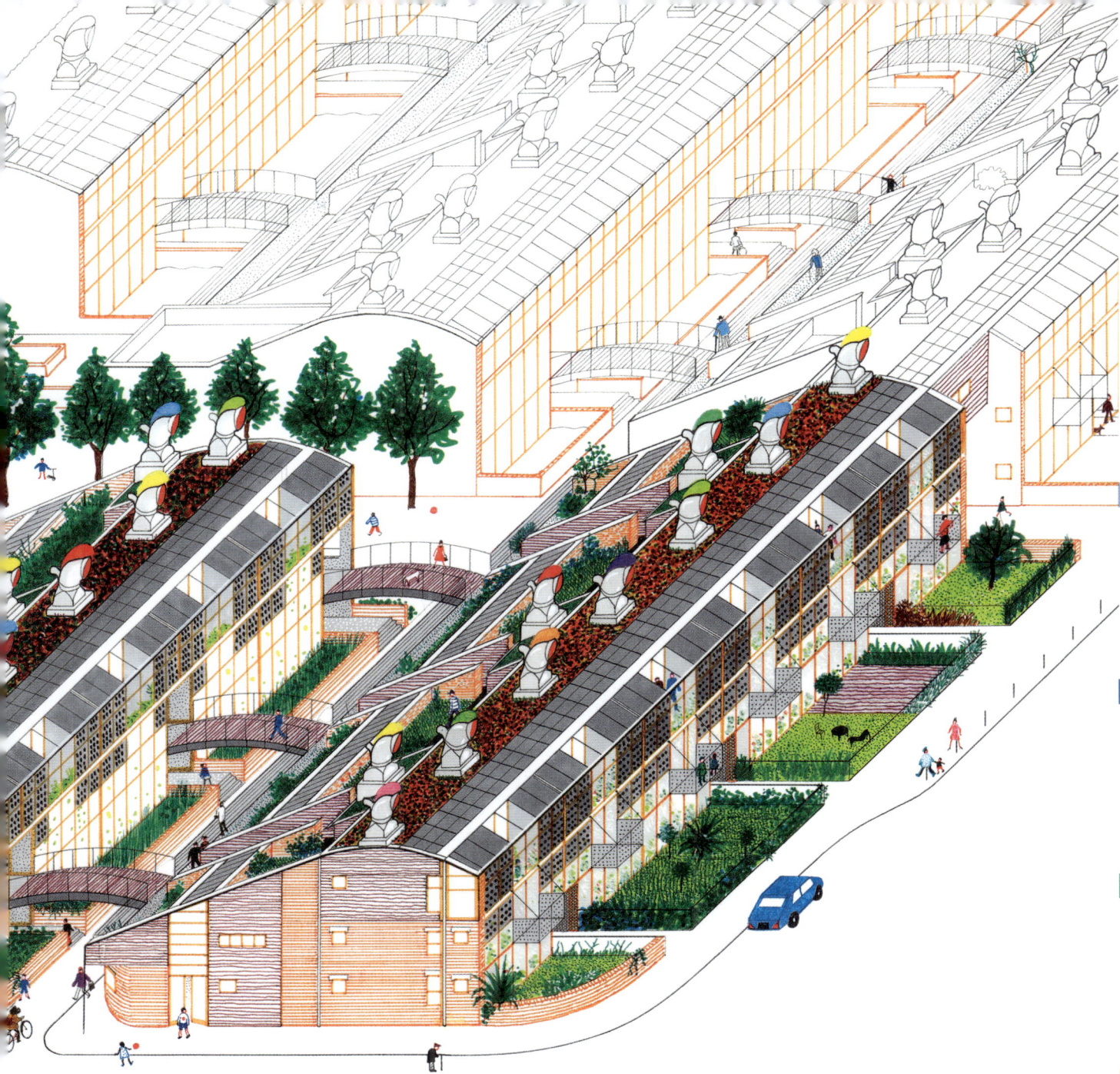

BedZED was built using local, reused and recycled materials wherever possible. The outside walls are covered in green oak from local woodlands, and the steel for the structure came from an old railway station. Roads were created using recycled glass sand (a sand created from crushed glass bottles), and the bricks for the walls were reclaimed from an old building site.

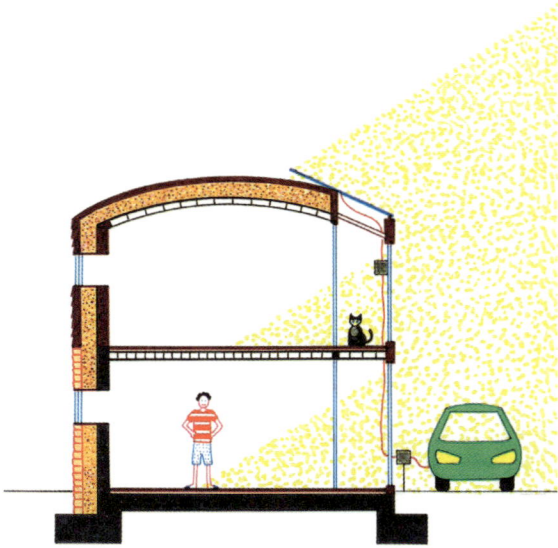

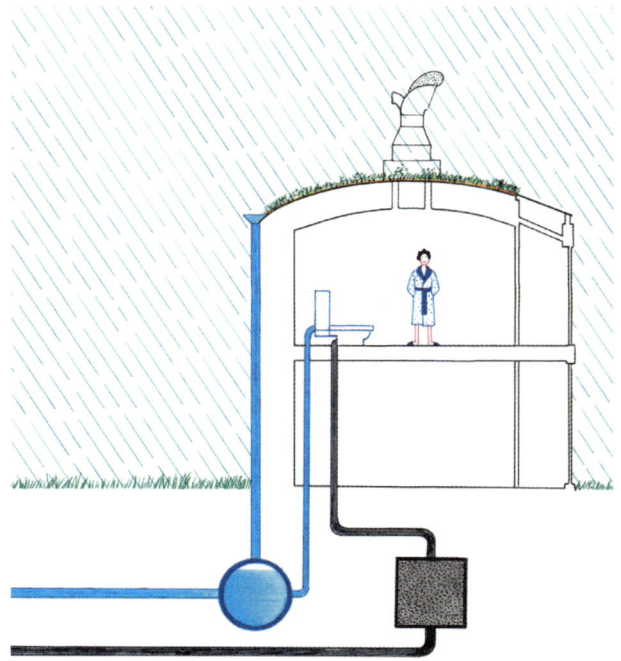

The houses are insulated against the cold and built facing the sun, which heats them and produces electricity. Rainwater is collected and purified using a natural filter system.

Having all the buildings in one place helps to create a sense of community. In this neighbourhood, with its school, studios and offices, everyone lives and thrives together.

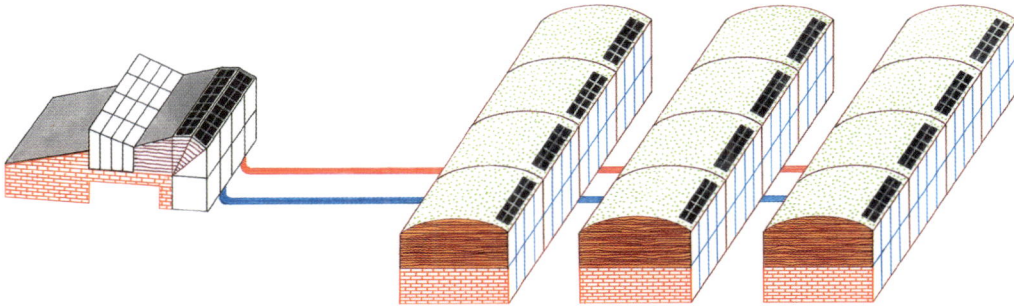

Nearby, a small heat and power plant that runs on green waste, like wood chippings, is used to power the community.

The wind spins weathervanes that are placed over openings in the roof to bring fresh air.

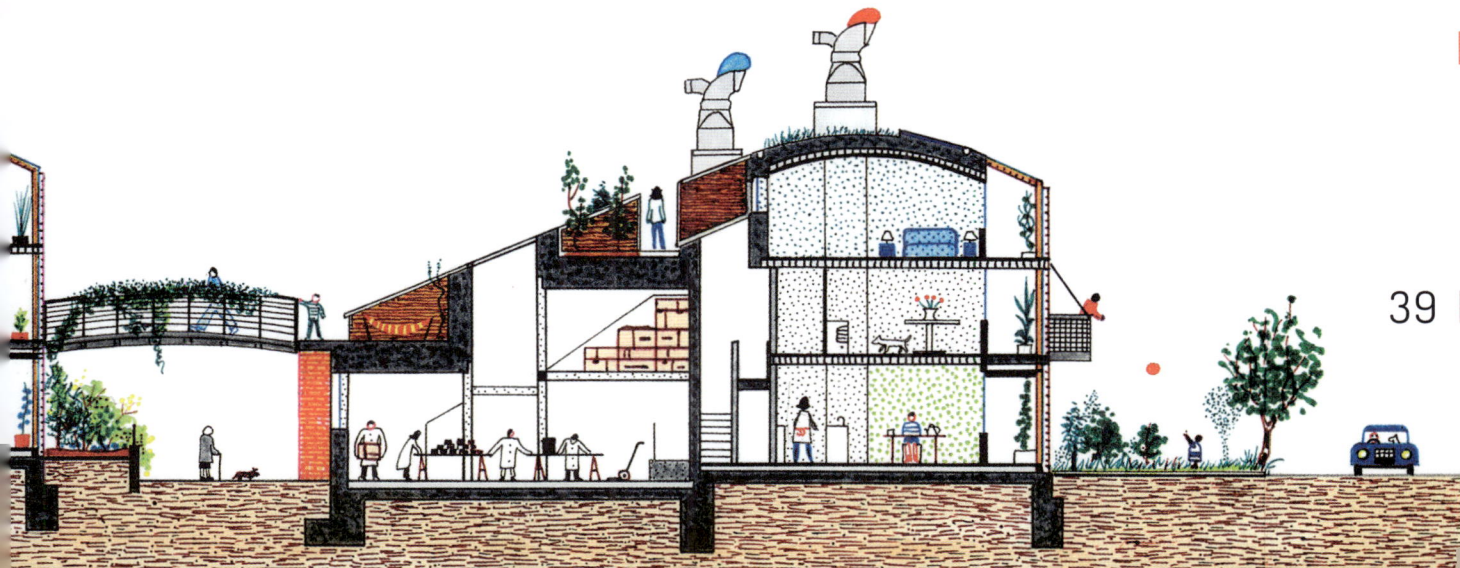

39

How Can We Get Around the City?

Large cities bring the challenge of transportation. A system is needed to help people travel, especially when walking isn't an option.

But it's not just within the city that the question of transport arises. How can we connect the suburbs and more remote towns to the city itself?

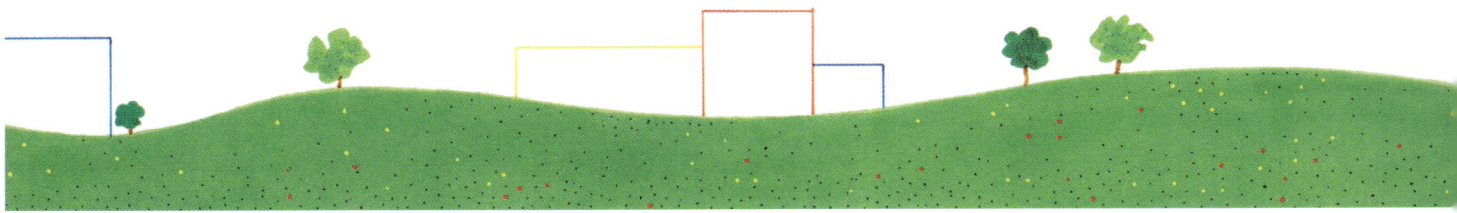

Initially, public transport was improved.
Then, new modes of travel were introduced ...

Extra-long, double bendy buses (270 passengers) and tube-shaped
bus stops in Curitiba, Brazil (1991)

CURITIBA: PLANNING WITH PEOPLE IN MIND

In the 1970s, the mayor of Curitiba in Brazil was worried that the city was expanding too far. He wanted to ensure people could travel around easily without relying on cars.

To protect the city's green spaces, building was limited and special protection was given to green areas. A priority bus service was created – the biggest in the world – which enabled everyone to get into the centre of the city easily. The bus service wasn't just for those that lived in the city, it would also stretch to more remote towns and would collect passengers from stops called 'tubes'.

But today, the growing population means that the city is once again struggling to stay green.

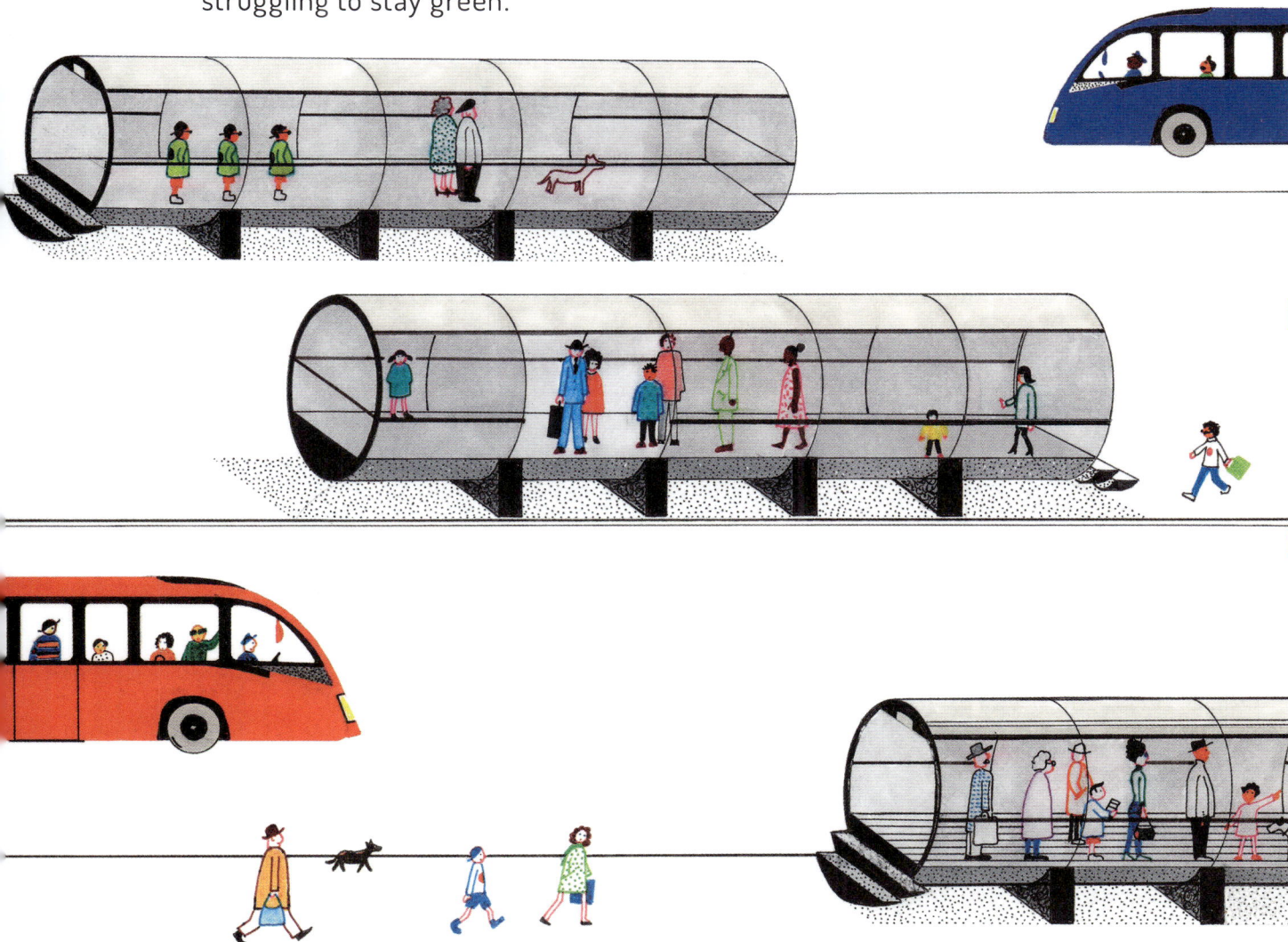

THE METROCABLE IN MEDELLÍN: A WELL-CONNECTED CITY

In Medellín, Colombia, the Metrocable whizzes up the steep hillside, high above the rooftops. Along the route, there are green spaces and libraries for passengers to visit. The idea of an affordable cable car came from discussions between experts, community leaders, local authorities and businesses.

Urban planning is a way of moulding the inner workings of a city to make it safe and accessible for everyone. This urban planning project delivered more than just a means of transport; it reconnected poorer hilltop towns to the rest of the city and helped support the development of those towns, leading to improved relationships between the people who live there.

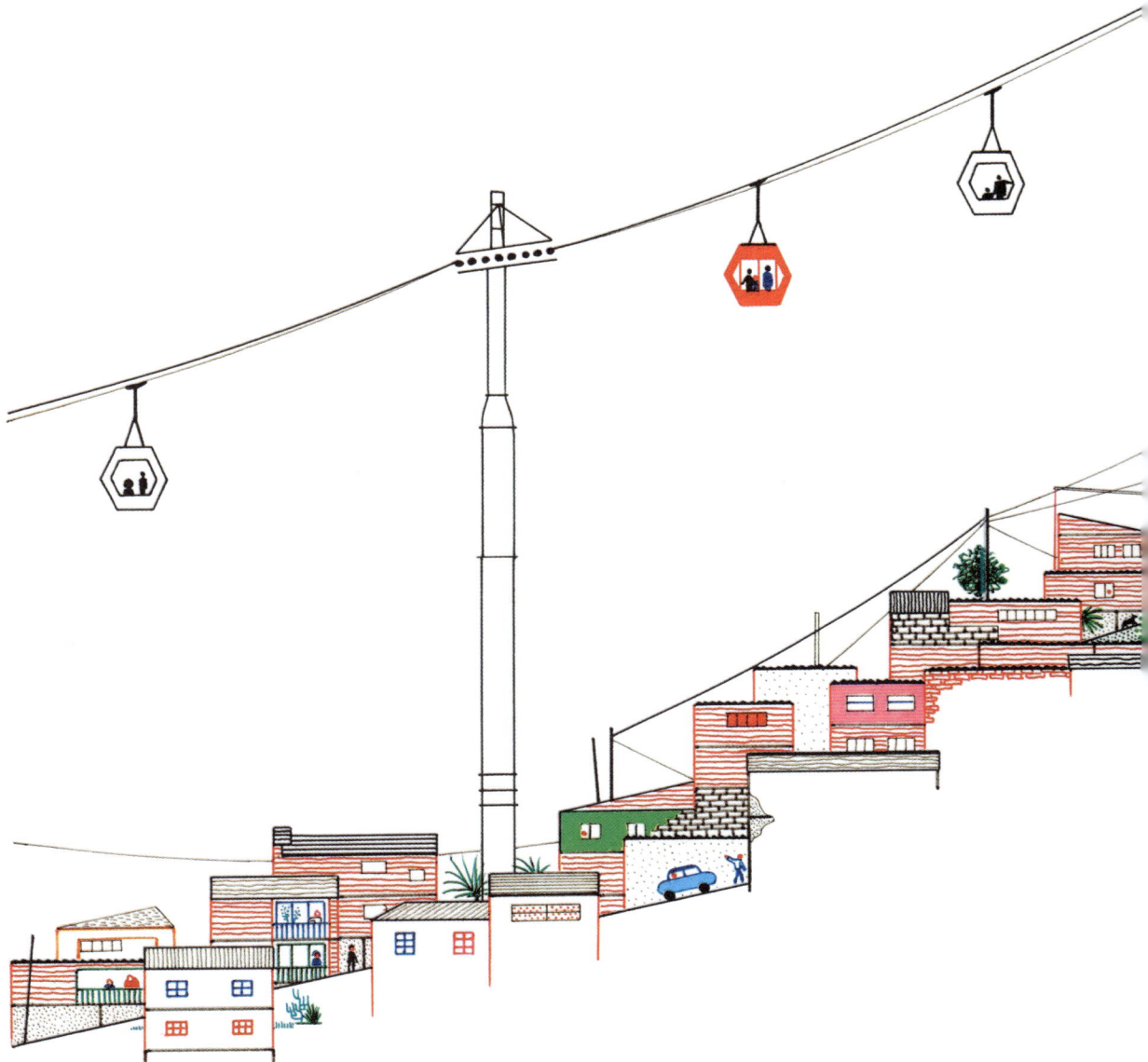

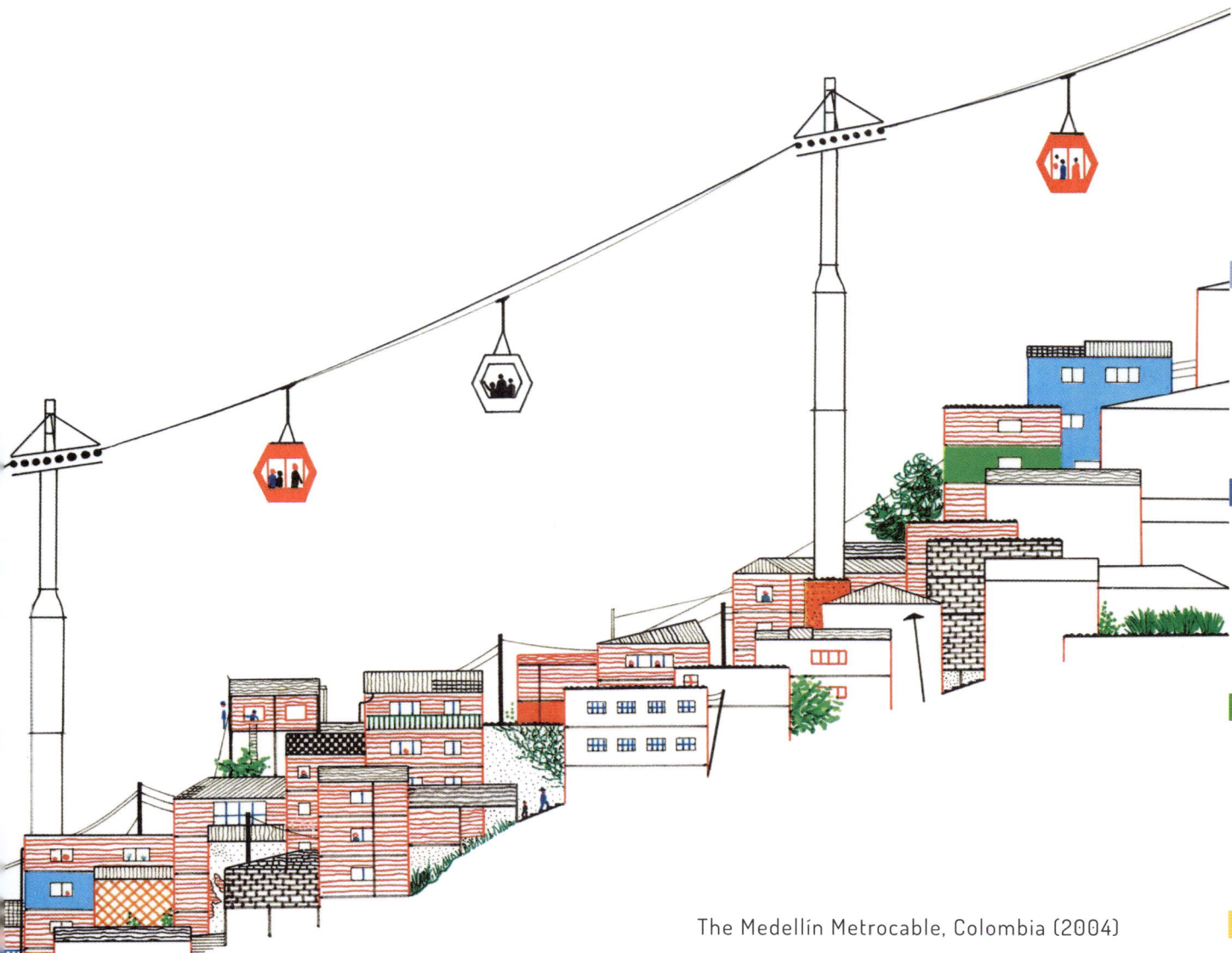

The Medellín Metrocable, Colombia (2004)

45

There are so many ways to get around in the city. Let's go!

At the end of the 19th century, some cities built in hilly areas (like San Francisco in the United States) chose tramways as a mode of transport. Now iconic, the open-sided cars are pulled by cables under the tracks and are still a convenient way to get around today.

The development of mobile phone apps has made it easier to arrange car sharing (several people travelling in the same vehicle). It's less expensive than travelling alone, reduces energy consumption and is a way of meeting new people. Many commercial vehicles are now electric, which means they cause less pollution and are almost silent which is perfect for a noisy, busy city.

Flying cars, like the Pop.Up, already exist as prototypes and might one day be on our roads! Imagine, some day in the future, we might be able to take off and fly over traffic jams!

The cable-operated tramway in San Francisco, United States (1873)

There are lots of wacky ways to get around, from unicycles to roller skates and scooters. But they have big competition: the Camioncyclette is part bike, part shopping trolley!

The Camioncyclette designed by Christophe Machet (2010)

47

The most environmentally-friendly way to get around is still on foot!

You'll find all kinds of clothing, safety gear and accessories for every type of bike ride. Remember to wear a helmet to stay safe!

COPENHAGEN: CITY OF CYCLING

In Copenhagen, half of all journeys are made by
bicycle. It's become a popular way for everyone
to get around – in fact, it's *the* way to get around!

Denmark's capital was once devoted to cars, but now bikes
have priority. The Cykelslangen (which means 'bicycle snake'
in Danish), is a cycle lane with a bright red surface which
is raised above roads and rivers. It twists through the air
between the buildings in the south of the city.

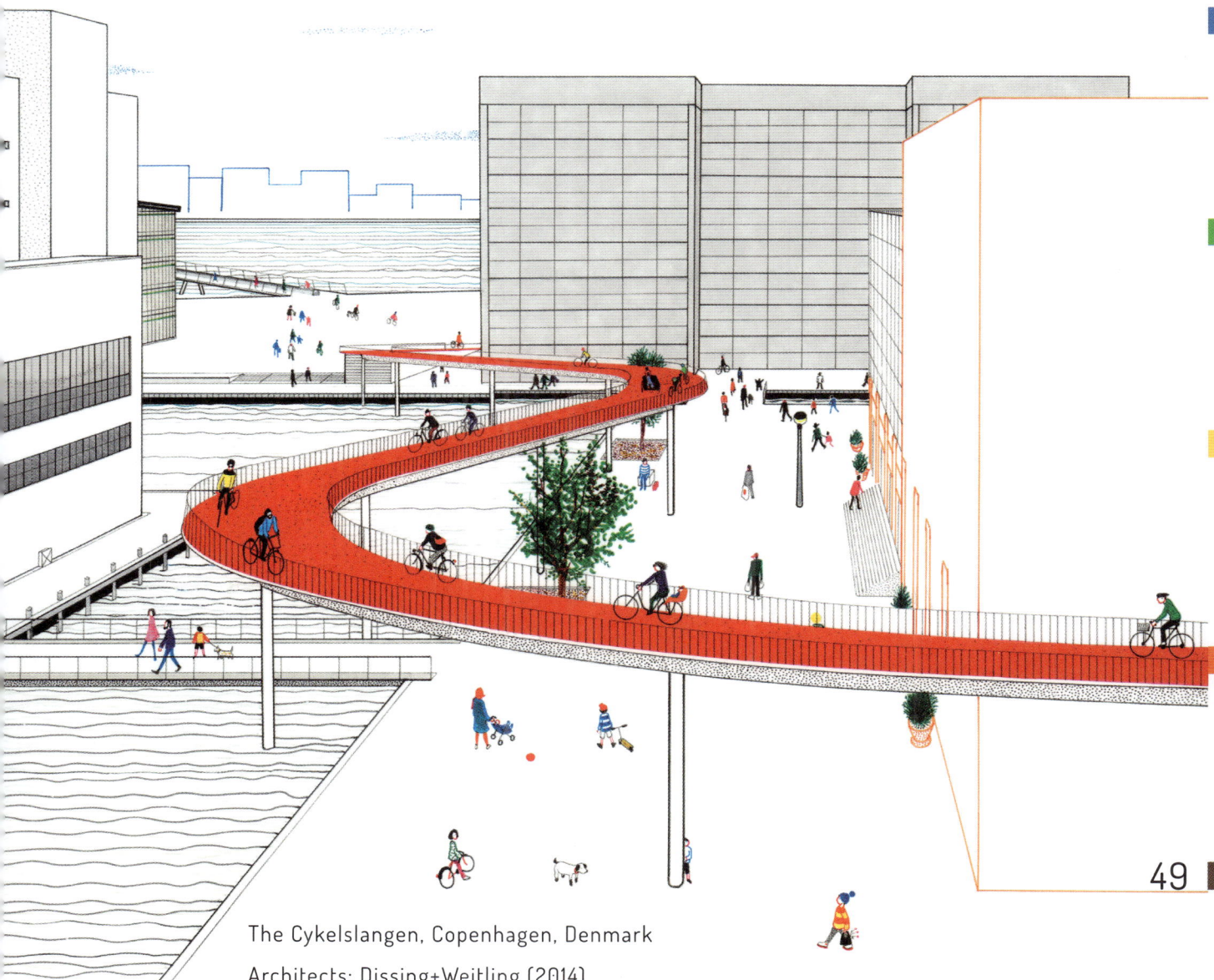

The Cykelslangen, Copenhagen, Denmark
Architects: Dissing+Weitling (2014)

49

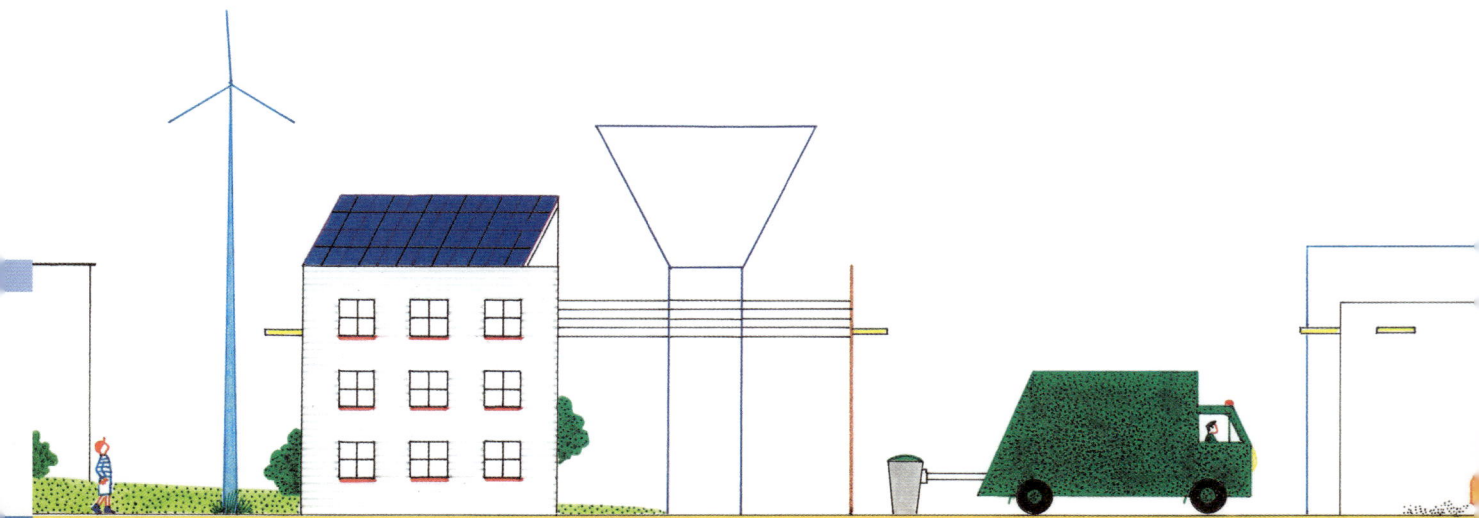

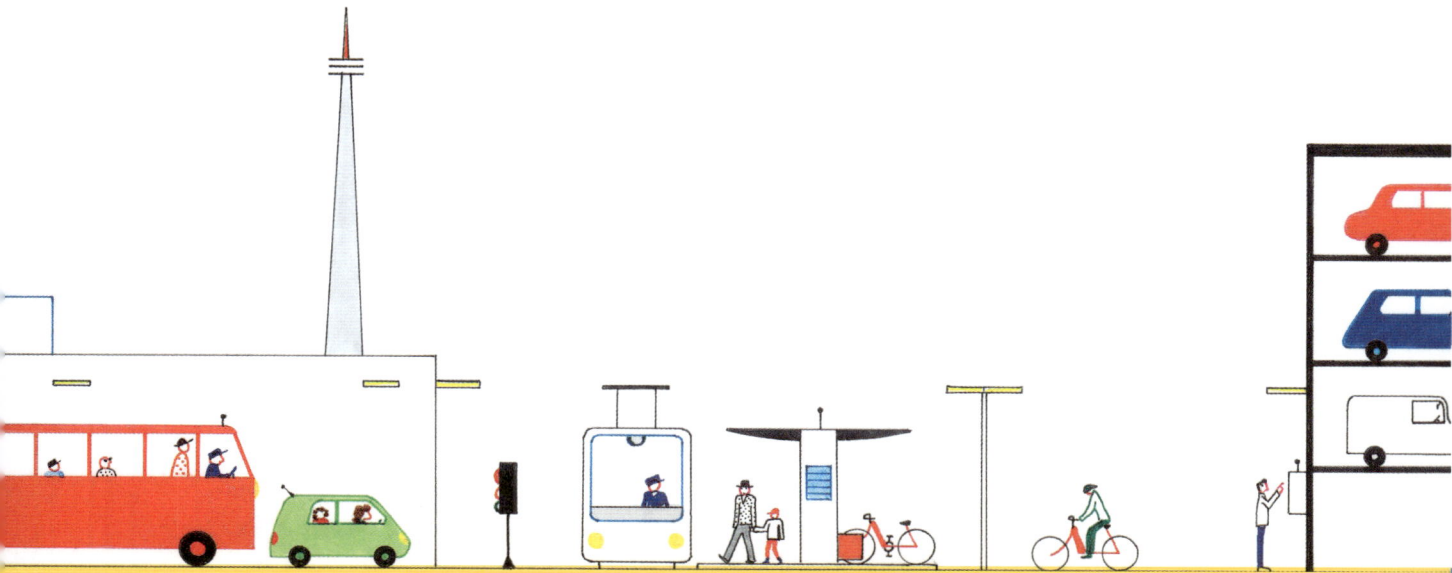

Can a City Be Smart?

A city is alive with movement. It's like a huge machine that's responsible for supplying energy, running schools and hospitals, getting rid of rubbish, controlling traffic and sharing useful information.

The city has to be responsive to the systems that run it and changes that can occur at any time of the day and night.

Singapore is installing sensors on its water pipelines, road systems and other networks.

The data is collected and computerised. This allows the city to have a connected system that can be viewed on screen, making it much easier to manage and control.

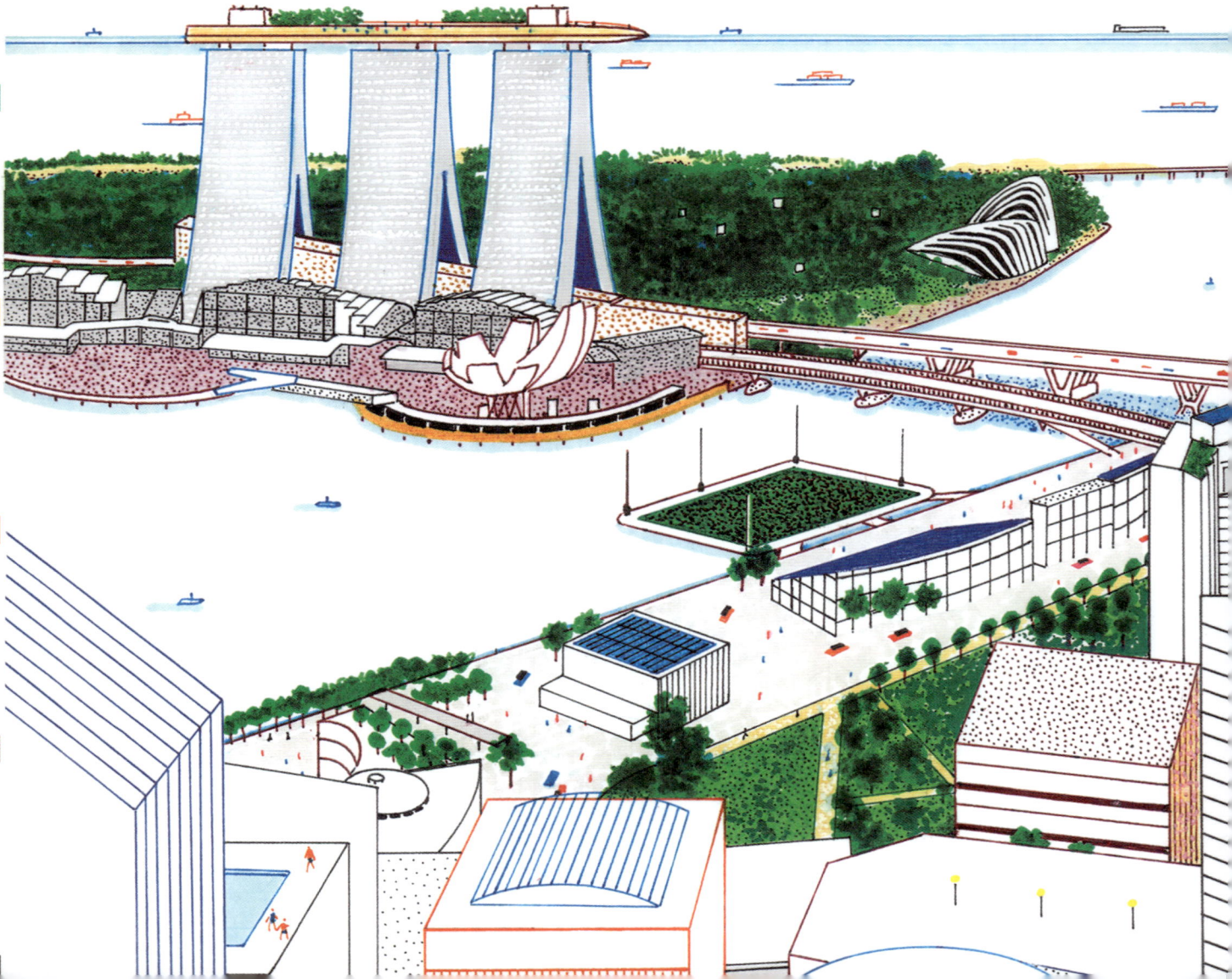

SINGAPORE: THE SMART CITY

When it comes to smart cities, Singapore is a world leader. The Smart Nation programme, launched by the government in 2014, fitted the city with a range of sensors and cameras. It meant that they could bring healthcare directly to the home, improve transport systems and reduce energy consumption.

The people of Singapore welcomed the benefits of the new system. One key advantage is that everyone can enjoy free transport during off-peak hours and reduced tariffs on toll roads (roads that require payment to use) if they travel at quieter times.

There are also smart systems like alarms in community pools that can warn if someone is in danger of drowning and devices that check on elderly people in case they fall or get sick. But while this sounds incredible, some people feel it invades their privacy.

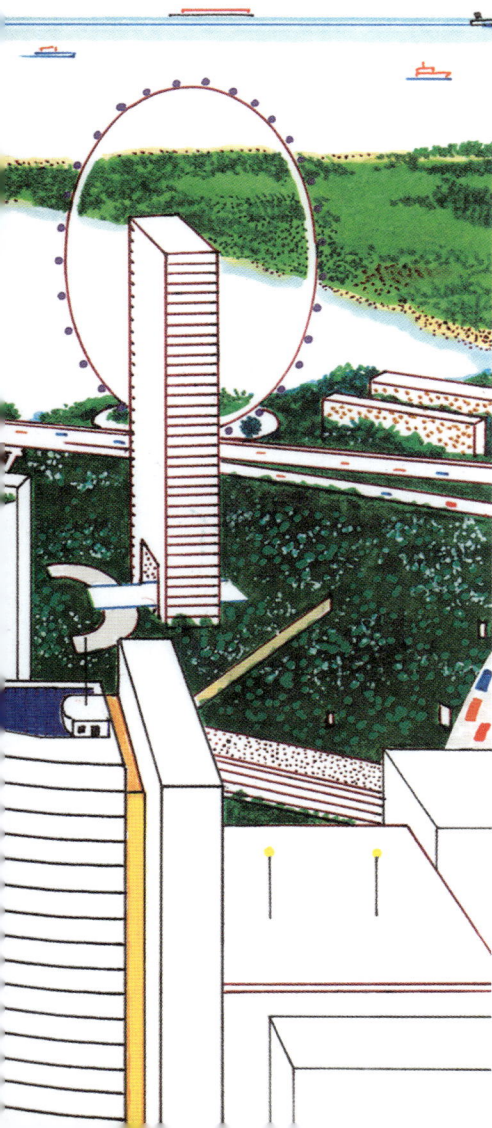

Marina Bay, Singapore

THE GARDENS BY THE BAY

Being a Smart City helps Singapore manage its resources and special care has been taken to protect the environment. The Gardens by the Bay project is a haven for biodiversity: plants, birds and insects. Giant smart glasshouses recreate different climates: the Flower Dome mimics a dry climate, while the Cloud Forest replicates the humid conditions of high mountain regions.

Over 250,000 species of endangered, rare plants are grown and protected there. The vegetation is lush and there's even a 35-metre-high waterfall!

Inside the park, Supertrees have been built. These enormous metallic structures stand between 25 and 50 metres tall. They're covered with plants which attract a number of insects and birds that go there to reproduce. The Supertrees are also used to collect rainwater and to harness solar energy.

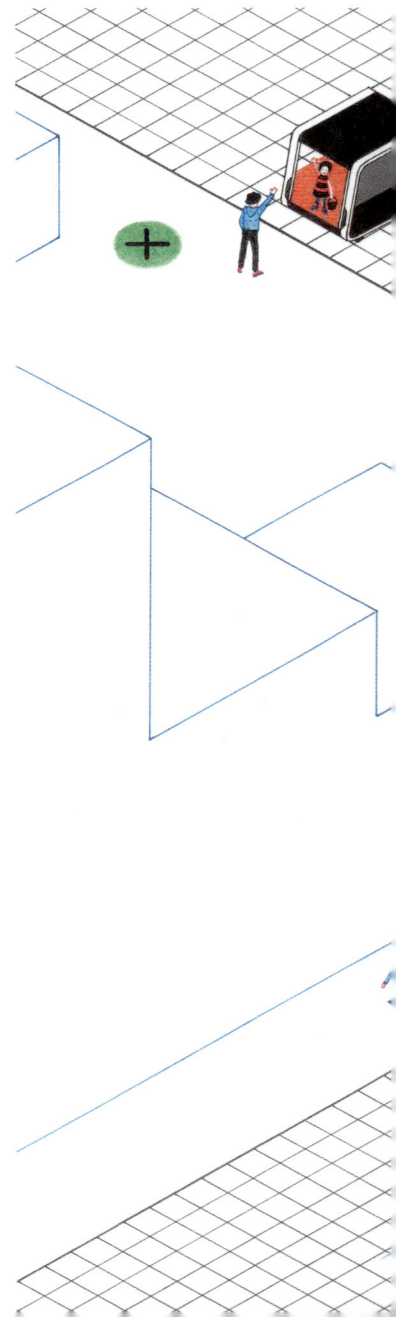

MODULAR TRANSPORT AND SELF-DRIVING CARS: THE TRANSPORT OF THE FUTURE

Physicist and designer Tommaso Gecchelin, founder of the company Next Future Transportation, has designed a self-driving car that can be programmed to take you wherever you want to go.

The cars can be attached to one another to create a sort of train – perfect for rush hour! Passengers can just sit back and relax. Gecchelin wanted to release the car in 2020, but faced challenges such as the structure of our cities and roads.

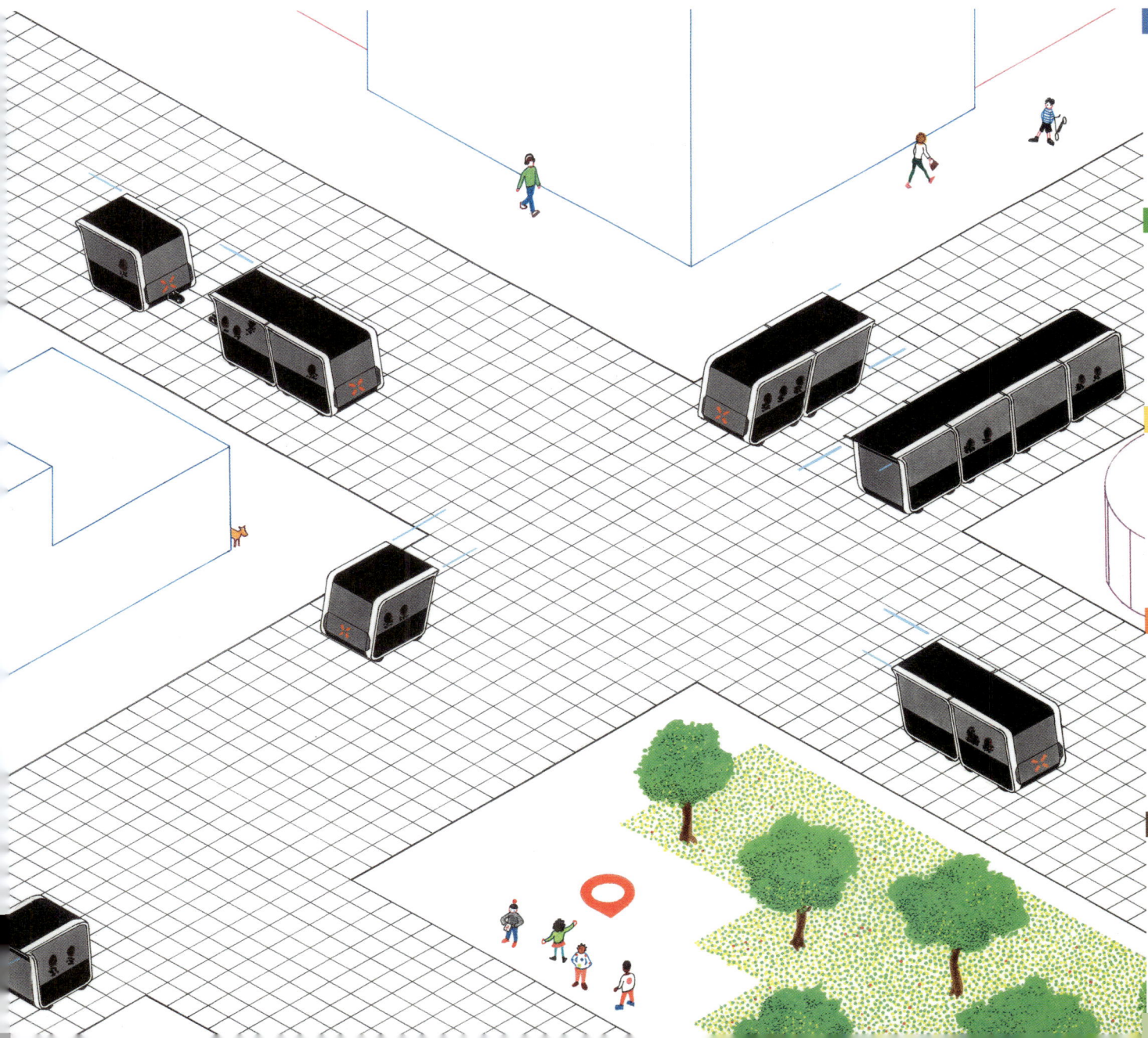

Working In the City

For decades, factories have been in decline and, more recently, shops on the high street are closing their doors as online shopping takes over.

What should we replace them with, and how can we ensure they create jobs? Can we create new opportunities and better ways of working together?

THE SOCIAL PALACE, GUISE:
AN UNUSUAL EXPERIMENT

The 'Familistère', or Social Palace, in Guise, France

Architect: Jean-Baptiste André Godin (1846)

When the industrial revolution took place in France in the 19th century, people started to look for ways to bring workers closer to the new factories that were springing up. They tried to design buildings that suited the workers' way of life.

Jean-Baptiste André Godin, who made cast-iron stoves, moved his factory to Guise in northern France in 1846. Godin believed in a fairer world and so he built a model city where he and his workers could live. He called it the 'Familistère', or 'Social Palace'.

The Social Palace included residential buildings, a nursery, a theatre, schools, shops, a laundry, swimming pool and a park beside the factory.

Godin created a cooperative, which meant he gave ownership of the Social Palace and the factory to the workers, so the workers could decide how it should be run.

The city was home to around 2,000 inhabitants, and there was a rich social life where neighbours would both work and socialise together.

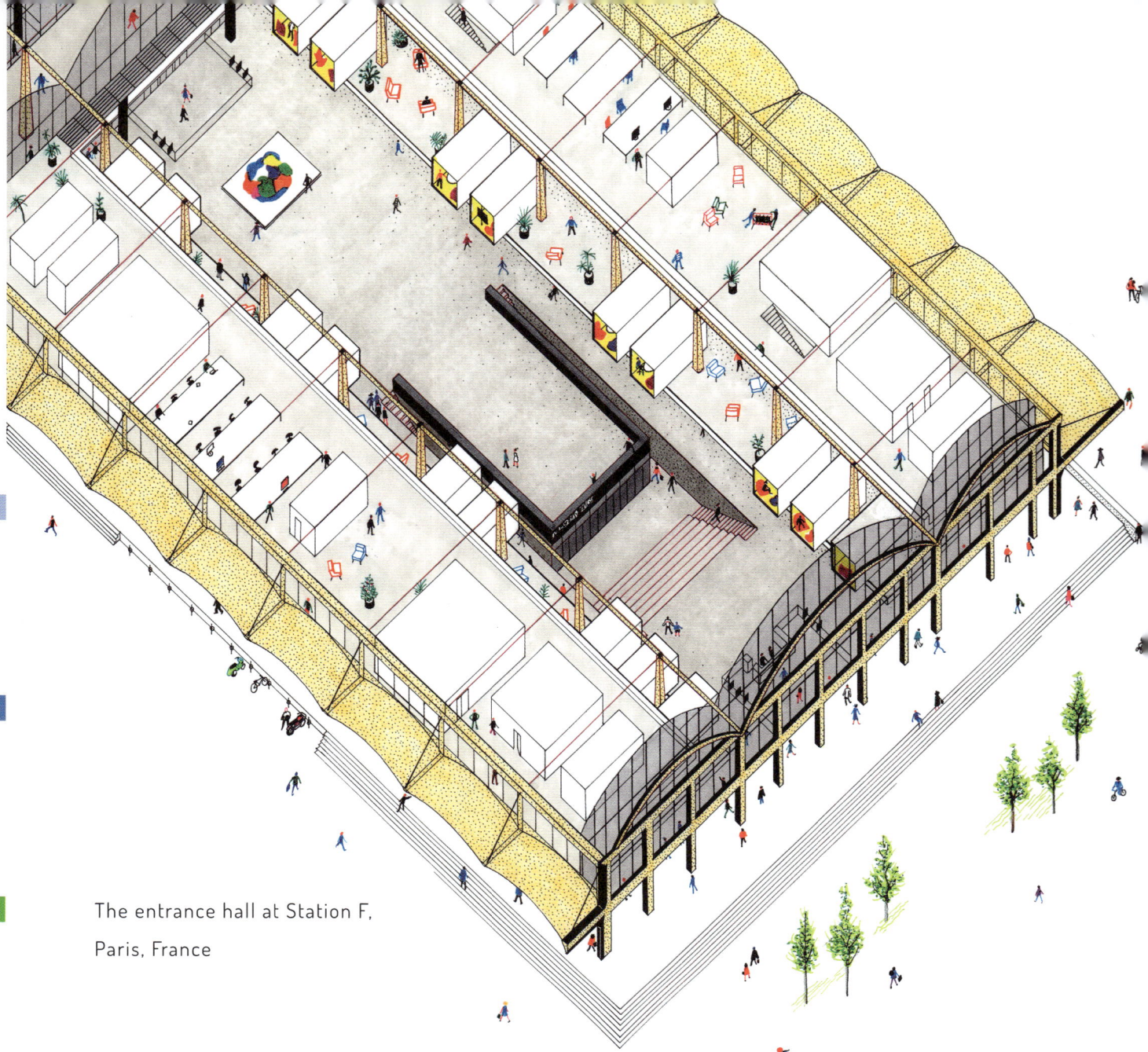

The entrance hall at Station F,
Paris, France

STATION F: BRIGHT IDEAS FOR BUSINESSES

In 1929, engineer Eugène Freyssinet built an enormous concrete hall near the Gare d'Austerlitz, one of the main railway stations in Paris. For many years it was used as a railway depot and was due to be demolished, but instead it was restored by architect Jean-Michel Wilmotte. He transformed it into the biggest centre for start-ups (young companies with exciting new products) and tech companies in the world. The original solid concrete structure has been retained, but the inside space has been completely redesigned.

To allow new businesses to grow at their own pace, 3,000 desks are available in shared working areas. Everyone has their own locker and people can work alone or sit with others around large tables or in offices. The architect created units known as 'villages' inside the building. The villages have their own small kitchens, drinks dispensers, toilets and comfy sofas, while shipping containers provide space for private meetings.

A vast entrance hall with a giant cinema screen (perfect for hosting events and presentations) completes the project.

The Freyssinet Hall, Paris, France

Built by Eugène Freyssinet (1929) and redeveloped by architect Jean-Michel Wilmotte (2017)

Mam'Ayoka in the 18th district of Paris, France (2016)

MAM'AYOKA: AN UNUSUAL OPPORTUNITY

Mam'Ayoka is a restaurant in Paris that's run as a cooperative. This means that it's owned and controlled by its employees. It offers work to women who find it difficult to get jobs, giving them a way to use their talents and earn a living. They prepare tasty recipes from their homelands such as couscous from Algeria or Tunisia, bao buns from Cambodia and fish dishes from Mali.

The dishes are served in the cooperative's small restaurant or delivered by bike to local shops and businesses. It's a small-scale business, but it helps everyone involved.

63

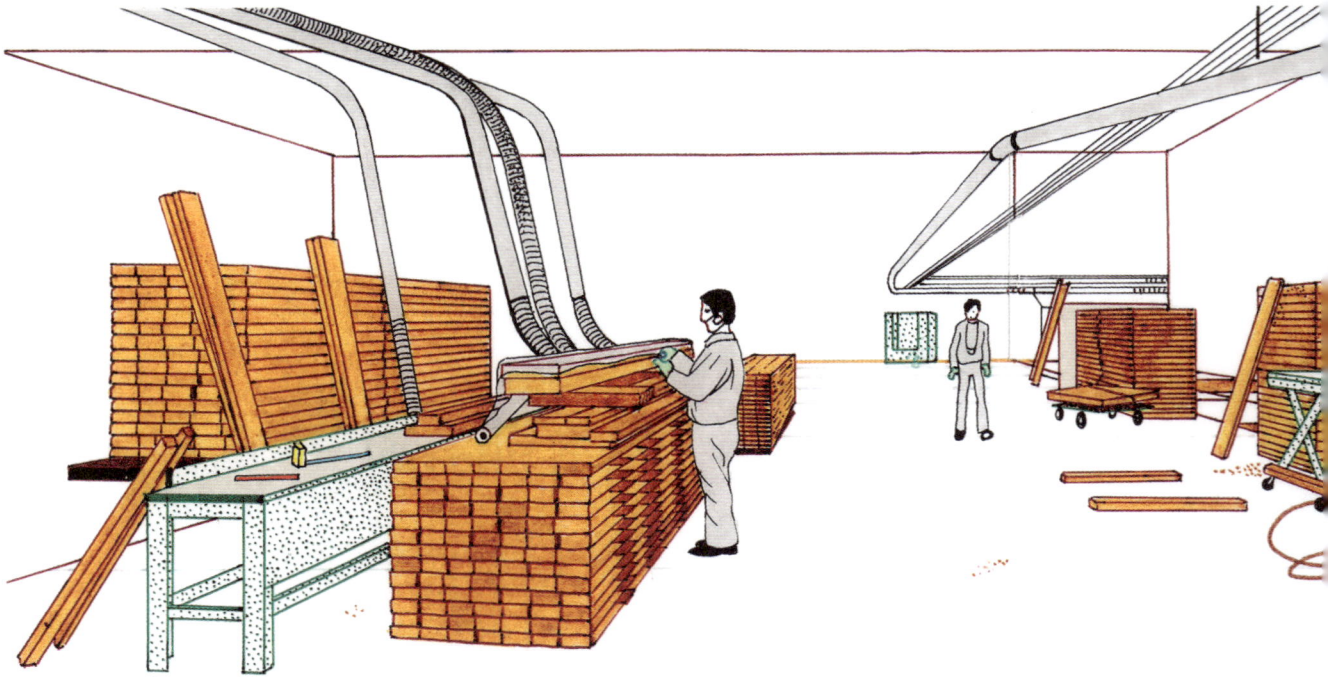

The Shimokawa Forest Family Company sawmill, Hokkaido, Japan

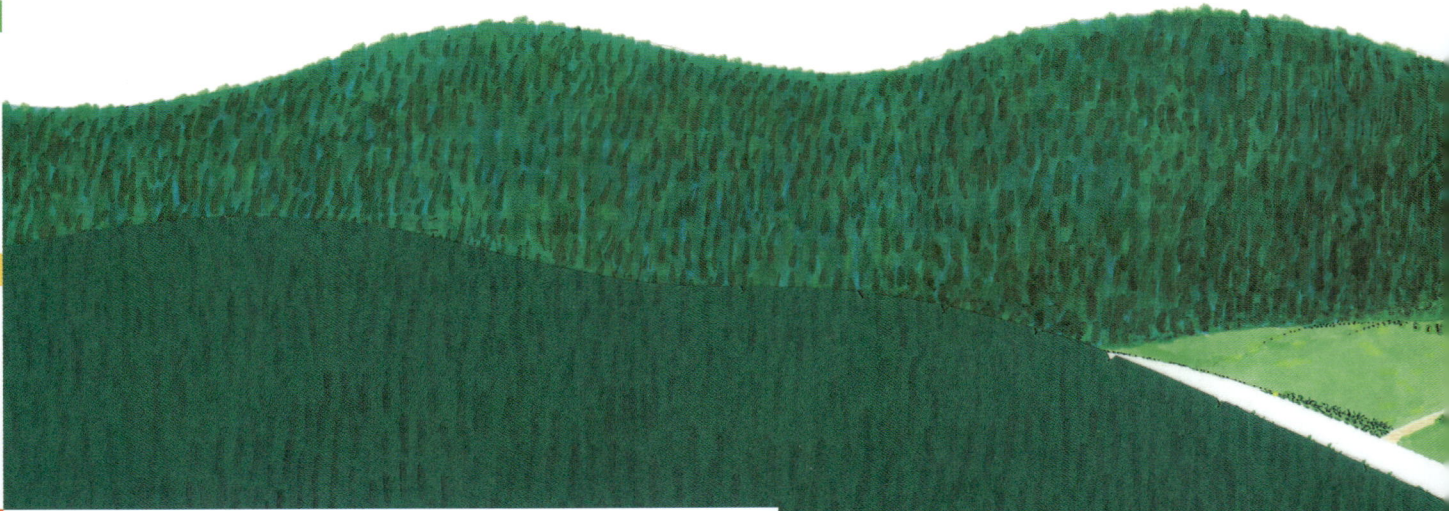

Greenhouses for young saplings in Ichinohashi

64

SHIMOKAWA: THE WOODLAND CITY

Shimokawa is a micro-town (a town that covers a small area of land and has a small population) on the island of Hokkaido in northern Japan that received support through the government's Future City programme. Surrounded by vast conifer forests, the town has focused on the forestry industry to support its ageing population.

A cooperative has been set up to produce laminated wood and develop new by-products from the leftover wood. The town also makes sure to take care of the forest by planting new trees to replace the ones they cut down.

The Ichinohashi collective housing area was built so that the island's older inhabitants could live together. A small heating plant burns waste wood to warm the houses.

The Ichinohashi collective housing area, Shimokawa Town, Hokkaido, Japan (2011)

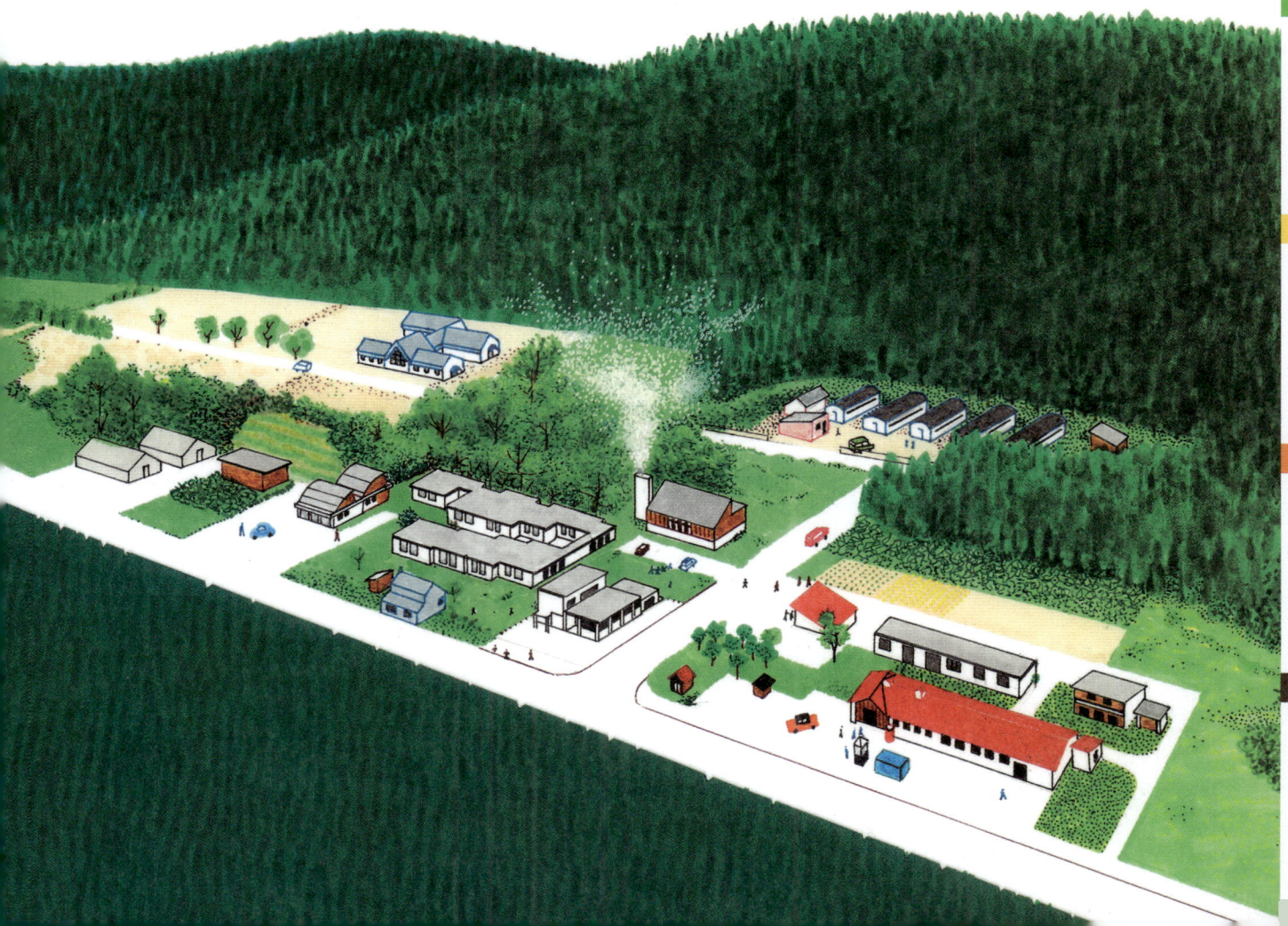

How Do We Create the City We Want?

Modern cities are often grey with dull streets and buildings that all look the same. But what if someone asked us what we think? If you could have your say, what might you create instead?

RIO DE JANEIRO: PROJECT MORRINHO

On the remote hills of this large city in Brazil, people have built their own houses without official permission. These towns are known as favelas. In this maze of narrow streets with their jumble of buildings, life can be hard.

Panorama of Project Morrinho during video recording
Favela Pereira da Silva, Rio de Janeiro, Brazil (1997)

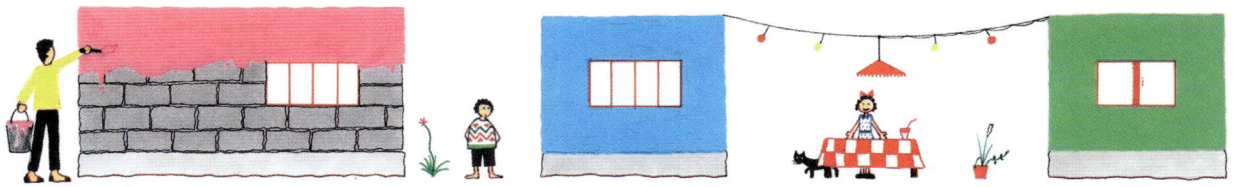

Houses in the favelas are basic and often looked down on. To show pride in where they live, a group of young people created an amazing, giant model of their town from bricks and other recycled materials.

Then, filmmakers showed them how to create their own recordings. The films they made showed the joys and hardships of city life. A TV channel was even created to broadcast them!

LAINGSBURG: LETTING THE PEOPLE DESIGN THEIR TOWN

In South Africa, architect Carin Smuts works with underprivileged communities and helps them decide how their town should develop. Many meetings and creative workshops are held to discuss exciting new projects for schools, sports halls and health clinics.

In Laingsburg, a town north of Cape Town, a poet has collected stories from the community. These include memories of a big flood that once happened there. To remember it, they created a long red abstract building.

Local trainees built a scale model out of sheet metal with the help of South African metalworker and artist, Willie Bester.

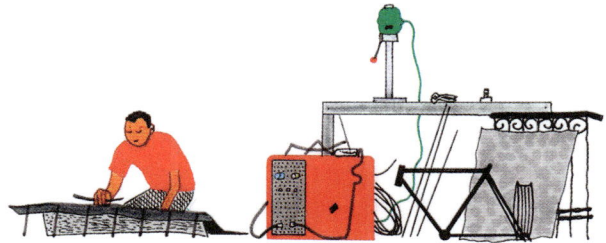

The Dawid Klaaste Multipurpose Centre in Laingsburg was completed in 2005. It was a hub that organised activities for local people and provided services to support the community. A giant windmill towered over it and an old railway carriage was transformed into a restaurant.

Can We Build a City That's Pretty and Welcoming?

Does a city have to be just a random collection of buildings separated by streets? Can we transform it into a wonderful place that people would never forget?

THE ELEGANT STREETS OF HAUSSMANN'S PARIS

In 1853, shortly after he took power in France, Emperor Napoleon III appointed Georges-Eugène Haussmann as his representative in Paris. He made Haussmann responsible for making Paris a cleaner and more attractive city.

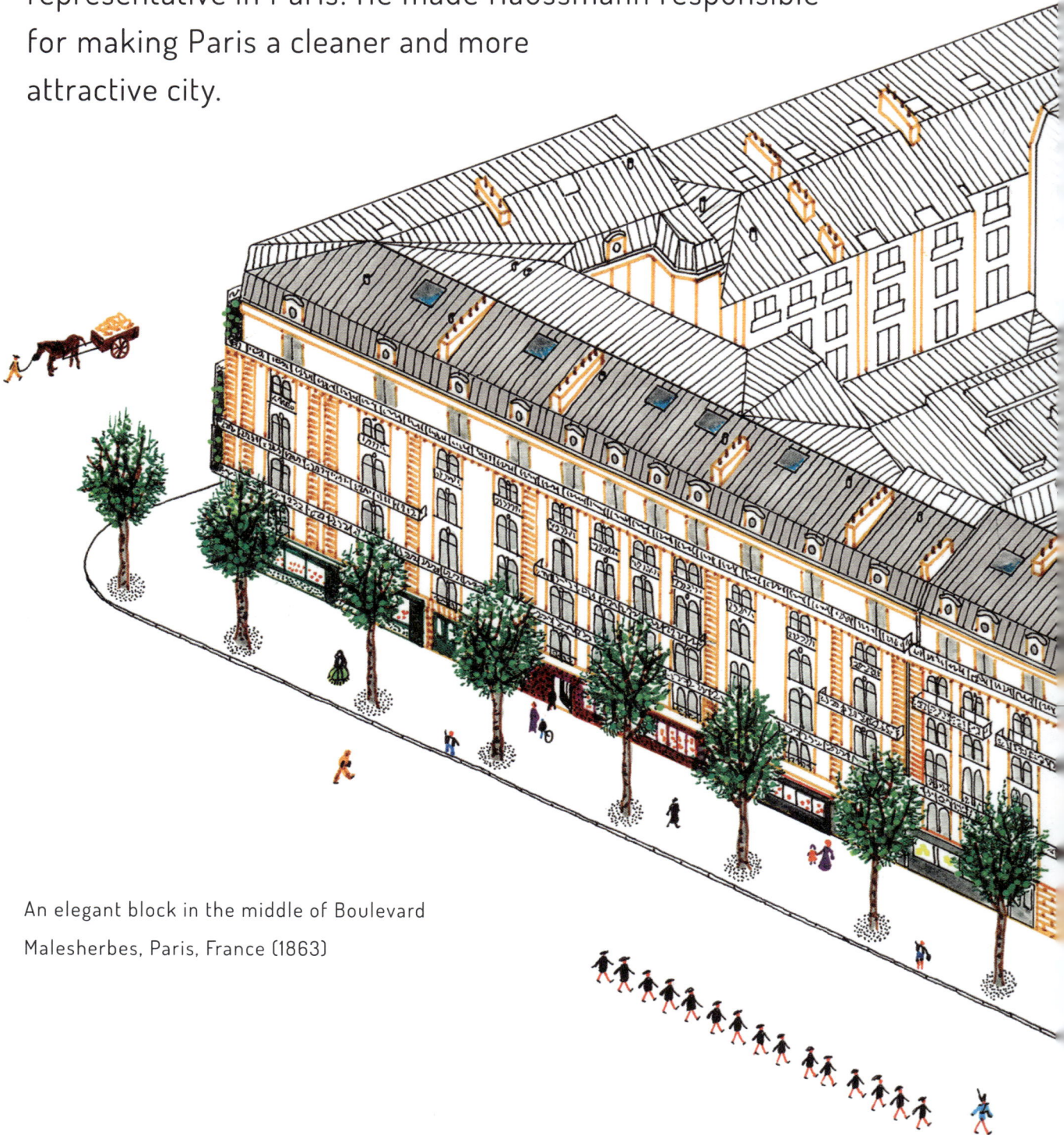

An elegant block in the middle of Boulevard Malesherbes, Paris, France (1863)

Haussmann tore down many of the poorer districts which often struggled with dirt and disease. In their place, he created wide avenues that cut through the city, meeting at its major landmarks. Elegant, tree-lined streets were built, together with beautiful parks and walks.

Strict rules were introduced: buildings in Haussmann's Paris had to be built of stone, conform to a specific style and include the same architectural features, such as long balconies. These constraints gave Paris an airy, harmonious appearance which inspired other great cities of the world, including Washington D.C. in the United States and Buenos Aires in Argentina.

THE POMPIDOU CENTRE: A REFLECTION OF THE TIMES

A hundred years after Haussmann's great redesign of Paris, another district of the city was transformed. This time, a densely populated part of Paris, shaped by the Middle Ages and the seventeenth century, embraced the ultra-high-tech form of the Pompidou Centre.

Using transparent plastic and metal pieces in primary colours, two young architects, Renzo Piano and Richard Rogers, brought pop culture to architecture. Their design includes a large piazza where people can meet, a museum dedicated to modern art and a relaxed library for students. This amazing building shows a new, modern way of thinking about culture. It was inspired by the exciting energy in Paris after big protests in May 1968 that changed traditional ideas.

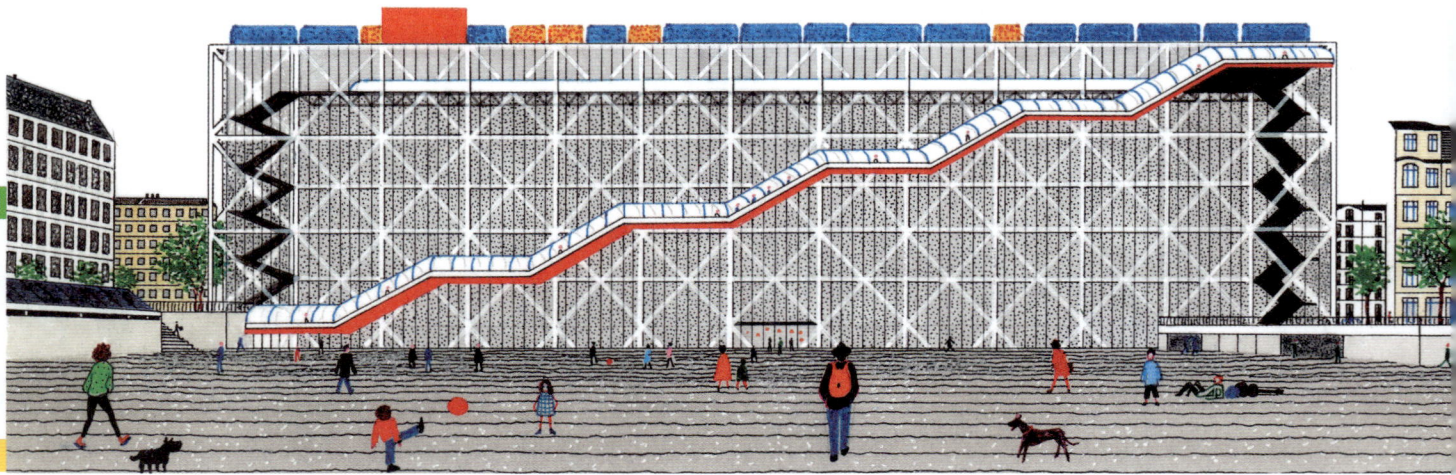

The Pompidou Centre, Paris, France

Architects: Renzo Piano and Richard Rogers (1977)

The Guggenheim Museum, Bilbao, Spain
Architect: Frank Gehry (1997)

THE GUGGENHEIM MUSEUM, BILBAO

In the 1980s, Bilbao, the capital of the Spanish Basque Country, was a gloomy, industrial town. But that all changed when architect Frank Gehry was commissioned to build the Guggenheim Museum there. The spectacular beauty of the museum transformed the city, attracting many tourists who helped it to flourish.

BORDEAUX: THE WATER MIRROR

Landscape architect Michel Corajoud has transformed the docks on the Garonne River in Bordeaux, France, into a wonderful place to stroll. The cranes and hangars have vanished. In 2006 the car park on Bordeaux's historic square, Place de la Bourse, was turned into a huge mirror reflecting the city's beautiful eighteenth-century buildings.

The Water Mirror, Bordeaux, France
Landscape architect: Michel Corajoud (2006)

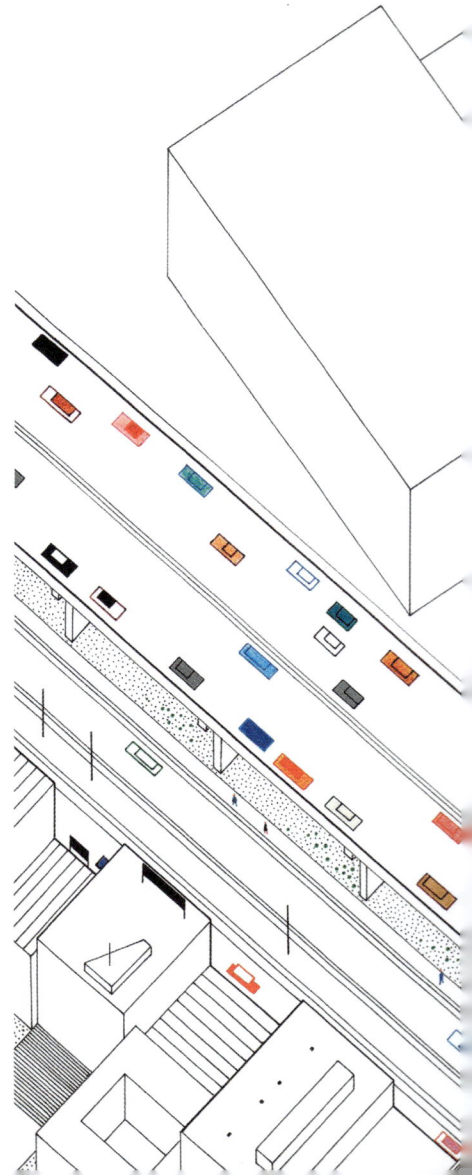

The Triangle Tower, Paris, France

Architects: Herzog & de Meuron (completion expected 2026)

THE TRIANGLE TOWER: A BOLD STATEMENT

Swiss architects Jacques Herzog and Pierre de Meuron were admirers of Haussmann's Paris and dreamed of building a new landmark for the capital. But why not put it in the outskirts instead of the city centre?

Their project, the Triangle Tower, is due for completion in 2026. The 42-floor building will be comprised of homes and businesses. Standing 180 metres tall, it will have a pyramid-shaped profile with glass walls.

Towering over the warehouses that line the motorway and the ring road, this bold building will be a clear sign that you're arriving in Paris.

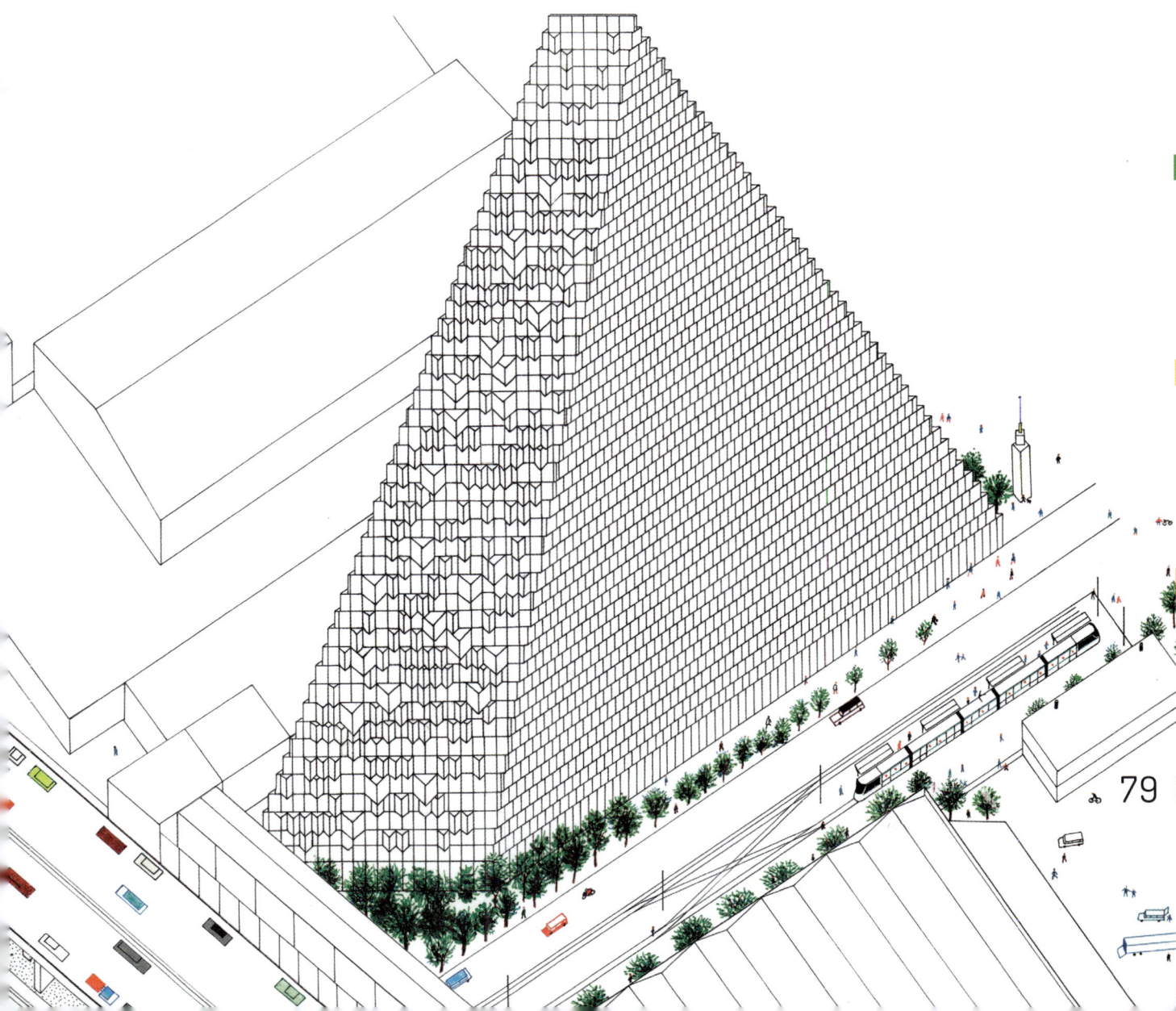

THE EMERGENCY HOUSING CENTRE IN IVRY-SUR-SEINE

In 2017, architect Valentine Guichardaz designed a welcome centre for refugees in Ivry-sur-Seine, a suburb of Paris, on behalf of the charity Emmaüs Solidarité.

Built on stilts on a former water treatment plant, it has accommodation, a school, social services and healthcare facilities. The complex is organised around a square where yurts serve as canteens, and there are also plans for a community garden. It has been made as comfortable as possible for refugees at this stage of their difficult journey.

City Living Is Great!

But shouldn't cities be places where everyone can come together and enjoy the best life has to offer?

SPACE TO PLAY IN AMSTERDAM

Architect Aldo van Eyck built many play areas
for children in Amsterdam, the capital of the
Netherlands, by repurposing empty spaces left
after the destruction of the Second World War.
On these plots, he designed areas with a mix of
surfaces made from different materials, simple
climbing frames, large sandpits, and a variety
of games – all aimed at helping children grow
strong and healthy.

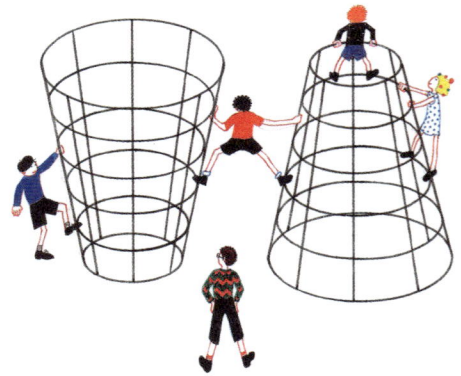

THE NEW YORK HIGH LINE

The High Line in New York, United States, has been a favourite spot for
many since 2009. The long, narrow park sits on top of a former railway
viaduct above the west side of Manhattan. Destined for demolition, it
was saved by local people and today is a popular place to walk, as well
as being home to a series of shared gardens.

From this aerial path you can enjoy a fantastic view of the streets
below and the Hudson River.

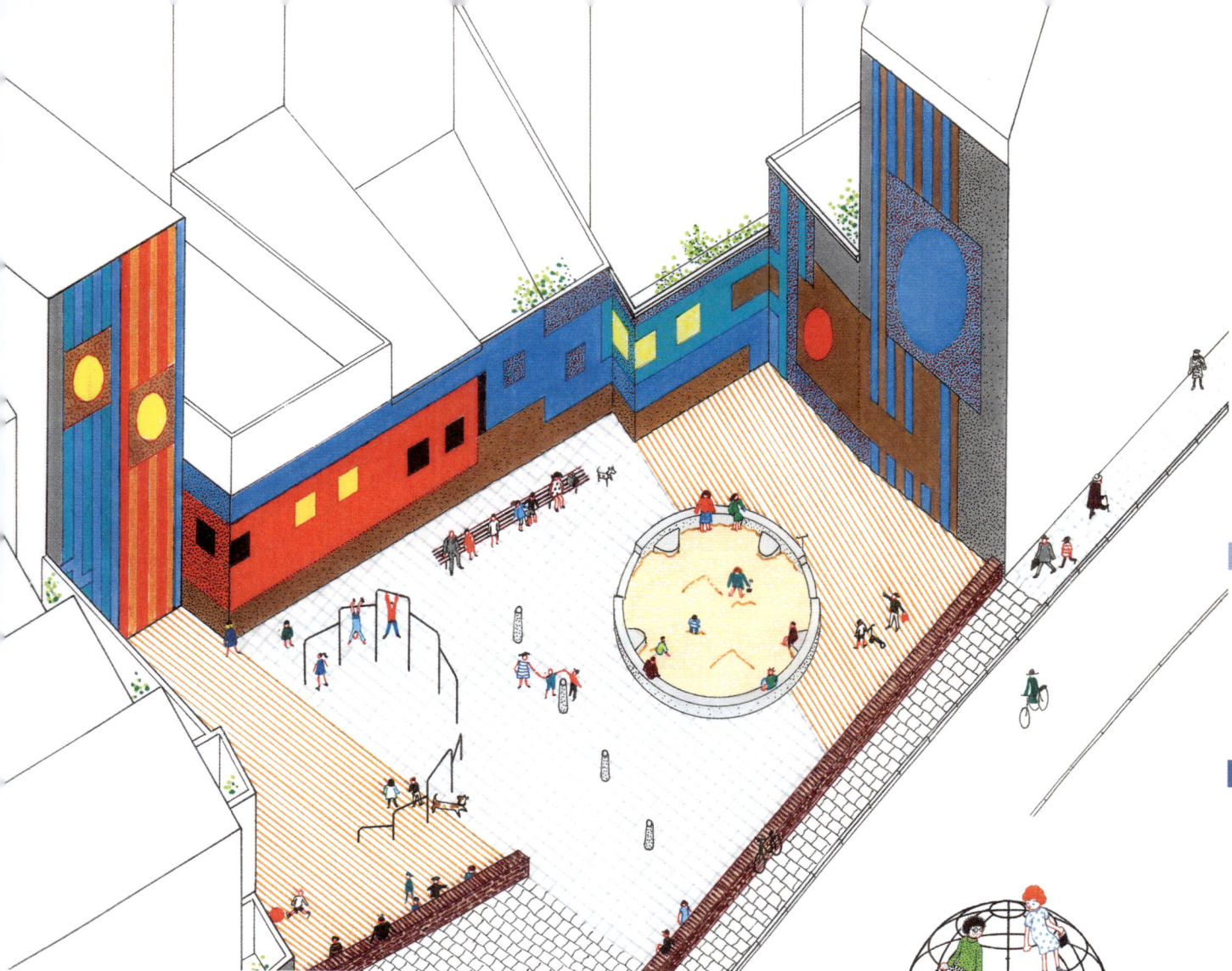

The playground in Zeedijk, Amsterdam, the Netherlands

Architect: Aldo van Eyck

Mural: Joost van Roojen (1958)

THE LX FACTORY IN LISBON

This former textiles factory on the banks of Portugal's Tage River has been converted into a trendy village full of restaurants, cookery schools, artists' studios and shops. Here you'll find the beautiful Casa Brasil, covered in huge street art murals painted by the artist Derlon, as well as one of Europe's biggest bookshops. Festivals and concerts are held here, and in the evening it's full of people enjoying themselves.

The LX Factory in the Alcântara district, Lisbon, Portugal (2008)